"If you read only one book this year, make it this one. It's that important." **Rick Warren**

the
Explicit
Gospel

Matt
Chandler

with Jared Wilson

"If you read only one book this year, make it this one. It's *that* important."
Rick Warren, #1 New York Times best-selling author, *The Purpose Driven Life*; pastor, Saddleback Church, Lake Forest, California

"This book, like the gospel itself, is clarifying, convicting, comforting, and compelling all at the same time. I wholeheartedly invite you to read it, to be overwhelmed by the mercy and majesty of God in the gospel, and then to spend your life making the gospel explicit in every facet of your life and to every corner of the earth!"
David Platt, best-selling author, *Radical*; Senior Pastor, The Church at Brook Hills, Birmingham, Alabama

"Matt Chandler is one of the best Bible preachers on the earth and one of the godliest men I know. I am thrilled to see this book released. Read it. And buy some extra copies to give away."
Mark Driscoll, pastor, Mars Hill Church, Seattle; President, the Resurgence and the Acts 29 Church Planting Network

"Too often the gospel fails to take root when it is assumed. The explicit gospel transforms individuals, churches, and nations as the mission of God is carried forward. Matt Chandler has gifted the church with a powerful tool to combat the assumed gospel. *The Explicit Gospel* is a serious threat to the moralistic, therapeutic deism that cripples the lives of so many. I highly recommend this book to both believers and unbelievers alike."
Ed Stetzer, President, LifeWay Research; contributing editor, *Christianity Today*

"That the gospel is not clearly taught in classic liberalism is disheartening but not surprising. That frequently the gospel is not taught in evangelical congregations is both disquieting and surprising. Evangelicals will not deny the gospel, but they may assume it while talking about everything else—and that is tragic. Matt Chandler issues a robust call to make the gospel an *explicit* and central part of our preaching and takes pains to show what that looks like. Amen and Amen."
D. A. Carson, Research Professor of New Testament, Trinity Evangelical Divinity School

"Matt Chandler presents the gospel in a way that is balanced, hope-filled, and very, very serious, all the while presented with Matt's trademark humor. Even more faithful than funny, Matt insults all of us (including himself) in a strangely edifying way, and in a way that I pray will make you treasure Christ even more."

Mark Dever, Senior Pastor, Capitol Hill Baptist Church, Washington DC; President, 9Marks

"*The Explicit Gospel* is a roadmap and wake-up call to our generation to grasp the full, expansive, and true gospel story. Matt is a leading voice, a great expositor of the Scriptures, passionate about Jesus, and serious about the gospel and making God known. When he speaks, I listen, and when he writes, I read. This book reflects the clear and core message of Matt's life, leadership, and passion for a generation hungry for truth."

Brad Lomenick, Executive Director, Catalyst

"People who come face-to-face with death make the best evangelists. I have to believe that's why my friend Matt Chandler is so passionate about a clear, biblical presentation of the gospel. Life is short. Eternity is long. May this book drive you to greater clarity in preaching the life-saving gospel of Jesus Christ."

James MacDonald, Senior Pastor, Harvest Bible Chapel, Chicagoland; radio teacher, *Walk in the Word*

The Explicit Gospel

Other Crossway books in the Re:Lit Series:

Gospel-Centered Discipleship, Jonathan K. Dodson (2012)

Rid of My Disgrace: Hope and Healing for Victims of Sexual Assault, Justin and Lindsey Holcomb (2011)

Redemption: Freed by Jesus from the Idols We Worship and the Wounds We Carry, Mike Wilkerson (2011)

A Meal with Jesus: Discovering Grace, Community, and Mission around the Table, Tim Chester (2011)

Note to Self: The Discipline of Preaching to Yourself, Joe Thorn (2011)

Community: Taking Your Small Group Off Life Support, Brad House (2011)

Disciple: Getting Your Identity from Jesus, Bill Clem (2011)

Church Planter: The Man, the Message, the Mission, Darrin Patrick (2010)

Doctrine: What Christians Should Believe, Mark Driscoll and Gerry Breshears (2010)

Scandalous: The Cross and Resurrection of Jesus, D. A. Carson (2010)

Leaders Who Last, Dave Kraft (2010)

Vintage Church: Timeless Truths and Timely Methods, Mark Driscoll and Gerry Breshears (2009)

Religion Saves: And Nine Other Misconceptions, Mark Driscoll and Gerry Breshears (2009)

Total Church: A Radical Reshaping around Gospel and Community, Tim Chester and Steve Timmis (2008)

Vintage Jesus (trade paperback edition), Mark Driscoll and Gerry Breshears (2008)

Death by Love: Letters from the Cross, Mark Driscoll and Gerry Breshears (2008)

the
Explicit
Gospel

Matt
Chandler

with Jared Wilson

CROSSWAY

WHEATON, ILLINOIS

Library of Congress Cataloging-in-Publication Data
Chandler, Matt, 1974–
The explicit gospel / Matt Chandler with Jared Wilson.
   p. cm.
   Includes bibliographical references and index.
   ISBN 978-1-4335-3003-6 (hc)
   1. Salvation—Christianity. 2. Redemption—Christianity. 3. Salvation—Biblical teaching. 4. Redemption—Biblical teaching. 5. Protestant Churches—Doctrines. I. Wilson, Jared C., 1975–   . II. Title.
BT751.3.C47   2012
230—dc23   2011036191

To Lauren

Not a day has gone by that I don't marvel at the gospel's work in you. Jesus's deep love for you, made manifest in both your passion for him and patience with me, is an evidence of God's grace on my life. I am more grateful than I can express to be walking this journey with you.

Contents

Introduction

The Gospel is the heart of the Bible. Everything in Scripture is either preparation for the Gospel, presentation of the Gospel, or participation in the Gospel.[1]

DAVE HARVEY

My concerns started on a Saturday night at a "Celebration Weekend" several years ago. Our church—The Village—was baptizing a great number of men and women who were publicly professing their belief in Jesus Christ as their Lord and Savior. As I walked into our small auditorium, I was greeted by a hefty man in his early twenties. He gave me a hug and then proceeded to tell me about a girl he had brought to hear the testimonies. With a bit of nervous glee in his voice he informed me that the girl was a witch, and he hadn't told her ahead of time where he was bringing her. A smile on his face, he told me she was really angry and he wanted me to know this "just in case something happened."

I sat down in the front row and with some anxiety prayed that God would give me wisdom if this thing turned into a scene from *Harry Potter: The Unrated Version*. I am a good interpreter of Scripture and a passionate man when it comes to the gospel, but when it comes to spells and curses and the manifestation of demons, I have enough experience to know I don't know enough and that I need more prayer, study, and discipleship (but that's another story for a different book).

About this time the screen that obstructs the baptistry was raised, and standing in the water were two women in their early thirties. Karen began to share her testimony.[2] She told us that for the last fifteen years of her life she had been heavily involved in the occult and witchcraft, and she began to list all the reasons Christ

11

was better, more powerful, and more loving than anything or any-one else, especially compared with what she had witnessed and been a part of in the occult. I breathed a sigh of relief and knew God was at work among us. A young man in his early twenties was next. He talked of atheism, alcohol, Buddhism, drugs, and doubt, and then he talked about how through the patience and persis-tence of a friend, the Holy Spirit had opened his eyes to the truth of life in Christ and forgiveness through his cross.

But the next four baptisms bothered me. One after another, each person stirred the waters and told some variation of the same story: "I grew up in church; we went every Sunday morning and night; we even went to Wednesday prayer, vacation Bible school, and youth camp. If the doors were open, we were there. I was bap-tized when I was six, seven, or eight, but didn't understand what the gospel was, and after a while I lost interest in church and Jesus and I started walking in open sin. Someone recently sat me down and explained or invited me to The Village and I heard the gospel for the first time. I was blown away. How did I miss that?" Or they would say, "No one ever taught me that."

I had heard all this before, but that night was the eve of the birth of our son, Reid. My daughter was three, and it hit me that my kids were going to grow up in the church. That night for the first time I asked the question, "How can you grow up going to church every week and *not* hear the gospel?" I quickly decided that these people had heard the gospel but didn't have the spiritual ears to *truly* hear it, to receive it.

Fortunately, the Holy Spirit wasn't going to let it go that easily. The question began to haunt me. I decided to have a few conver-sations and interviews with what we have called the "dechurched" men and women attending The Village. A few of them confirmed that my hunch was correct. They could go back and read journals and sermon notes from when they were teenagers or college stu-dents and see that they had indeed heard the gospel. However, what alarmed me most was the number of men and women who couldn't do that. Their old journals and student Bibles were filled with what Christian Smith in his excellent book *Soul Searching* called "Christian Moralistic Therapeutic Deism."[3]

The idea behind moral, therapeutic deism is that we are able to earn favor with God and justify ourselves before God by virtue of our behavior. This mode of thinking is religious, even "Christian" in its content, but it's more about self-actualization and self-fulfillment, and it posits a God who does not so much intervene and redeem but basically hangs out behind the scenes, cheering on your you-ness and hoping you pick up the clues he's left to become the best you you can be.

The moralistic, therapeutic deism passing for Christianity in many of the churches these young adults grew up in includes talk about Jesus and about being good and avoiding bad—especially about feeling good about oneself—and God factored into all of that, but the gospel message simply wasn't there. What I found was that for a great many young twentysomethings and thirtysomethings, the gospel had been merely *assumed*, not taught or proclaimed as central. It hadn't been explicit.[4]

Nothing New

This assumption has historical precedent. We can read about it in the pages of Scripture and in chronicles of church history. Consider these words from Paul in 1 Corinthians 15:1–4:

> Now I would remind you, brothers, of the gospel I preached to you, which you received, in which you stand, and by which you are being saved, if you hold fast to the word I preached to you— unless you believed in vain. For *I delivered to you as of first importance what I also received: that Christ died for our sins in accordance with the Scriptures, that he was buried, that he was raised on the third day in accordance with the Scriptures.*

Paul is reminding the Christians of the gospel. He's saying, "Don't forget it! You were saved by it, will be sustained by it, and are currently standing in it."

For some reason—namely, our depravity—we have a tendency to think that the cross saves us from past sin, but after we are saved, we have to take over and clean ourselves up. This sort of thinking is devastating to the soul. We call this the "assumed gospel," and it flourishes when well-meaning teachers, leaders, and preachers set out to see lives first and foremost conformed to a pattern of behavior (religion) and not transformed by the Holy Spirit's power (gospel). The apostle Paul saw this bad teaching and practice happen often, and he went on the offensive against it:

> I am astonished that you are so quickly deserting him who called you in the *grace of Christ* and are turning to a different gospel—not that there is another one, but there are *some who* trouble you and want to distort the gospel of Christ. But even if we or an angel from heaven should preach to you a gospel contrary to the one we preached to you, let him be accursed. As we have said before, so now I say again: If anyone is preaching to you a gospel contrary to the one you received, let him be accursed. (Gal. 1:6–9)

> I have been crucified with Christ. It is no longer I who live, but Christ who lives in me. And the life I now live in the flesh I live by faith in the Son of God, who loved me and gave himself for me. I do not nullify the grace of God, for if righteousness were through the law, then Christ died for no purpose. O foolish Galatians! Who has bewitched you? It was before your eyes that Jesus Christ was publicly portrayed as crucified. Let me ask you only this: *Did you receive the Spirit by works of the law or by hearing with faith? Are you so foolish? Having begun by the Spirit, are you now being perfected by the flesh?* Did you suffer so many things in vain—if indeed it was in vain? Does he who supplies the Spirit to you and works miracles among you do so by works of the law, or by hearing with faith? (Gal. 2:20–3:5)

The idolatry that exists in man's heart always wants to lead him away from his Savior and back to self-reliance no matter how pitiful that self-reliance is or how many times it has betrayed him. Religion is usually the tool the self-righteous man uses to exalt himself. Again, this isn't new; the apostle Paul lays out in Philippians 3:4–9 his religious pedigree and practice as an example of what a man can accomplish with discipline and hard work. In that passage Paul states that all his religious effort, exhaustive checklist of all his accomplishments included, amounts to nothing compared to the surpassing greatness of Christ. He goes a step further and even calls it "rubbish" or "dung."

Think about that: all your church attendance, all your religious activities, your Sunday school attendance medals, your journals, having a "quiet time," reading the Scriptures—it's all in vain if you don't have Christ. When you read Paul's texts together, you get a feel for his attack on the Christian, moralistic, therapeutic deism of his day. We are saved, sanctified, and sustained by what Jesus did for us on the cross and through the power of his resurrection. If you add to or subtract from the cross, even if it is to factor in biblically mandated religious practices like prayer and evangelism, you rob God of his glory and Christ of his sufficiency. Romans 8:1 tells us that there is no condemnation for us, not because of all the great stuff we've done but because Christ has set us free from the law of sin and death. My sin in the past: forgiven. My current struggles: covered. My future failures: paid in full all by the marvelous, infinite, matchless grace found in the atoning work of the cross of Jesus Christ.

Gospel?

I have been encouraged and emboldened by the number of cries for gospel-centered ministry occurring in evangelicalism. From books to blogs, conferences to DVDs, there is a call back to what is of "first importance" (1 Cor. 15:3). But I want to spend my time with you trying to make sure that when we use the word *gospel*, we are talking about the same thing. Unfortunately there are, as you have seen referenced in Paul's writings, false gospels. I want to make sure we are all on the same page here—which is to say, God's page—and talking about what *he* is talking about when the gospel is mentioned in the Scriptures.

The Bible establishes two frames of reference for the same gospel. I call these vantage points the "ground" and the "air," and in this book we're going to see how together, they comprise the explicit gospel. In part 1, "The Gospel on the Ground," we will trace the biblical narrative of God, Man, Christ, Response. Here we will see the power of grace for human transformation. Beginning with God's endless self-sufficiency and culminating in a sinner's Spirit-abled response to the good news, we'll see how the glory of God reigns supreme over every plot point in God's plan for man. When we consider the gospel from the ground, we see clearly the work of the cross in our lives and the lives of those around us, the capturing and resurrecting of dead hearts. We see the gospel extended in this way when Jesus and his prophets call individuals to repent and believe.

When we get to part 2, "The Gospel in the Air," we'll see how the apostle Paul connects human salvation to cosmic restoration in Romans 8:22–23. Here we'll look at the oft-forgotten meta-narrative of the Bible's story of redemption. Paul writes:

> For we know that the whole creation has been groaning together in the pains of childbirth until now. And not only the creation, but we ourselves, who have the firstfruits of the Spirit, groan inwardly as we wait eagerly for adoption as sons, the redemption of our bodies.

If the gospel on the ground is the gospel at the micro level, the gospel in the air is the story at the macro level. Here we find a tour de force story of creation, fall, reconciliation, consummation—a grand display of God's glory in his overarching purposes of subjecting all things to the supremacy of Christ. As we examine the gospel in the air, we'll see from the scriptural testimony of Jesus's atoning work that the gospel is not just personal, but cosmic. When we consider the gospel from the air, the atoning work of Christ culminates and reveals to us the big picture of God's plan of restoration from the beginning of time to the end of time and the redemption of his creation. We may see the gospel extended this way in Jesus's declaration in Revelation 21:5, that he is "making all things new."

We see these two vantage points positioned together in Romans 8:22–23. In this passage we see that the gospel is the fulfillment of the longing of all of fallen creation but also (and chiefly) the fulfillment of the longing of mankind, the only creature made in God's image.

One gospel, two vantage points. Both are necessary in order to begin to glimpse the size and the weight of the good news, the eternity-spanning wonderment of the finished work of Christ. Both are necessary so that we are not reductionistic in how we define what God is up to both in our hearts and in the universe around us. If the gospel is reduced because of our preferences or misunderstandings, we leave ourselves open to heresies and to attacking our brothers-in-arms.

Most of the time, each of us views the same glorious truth from a particular vantage point. It might help to think about how someone walking down a New York City block sees the city versus how someone flying 30,000 feet overhead sees it. Both would say, "This is New York," and both would be right. What a silly argument the two would have if they tried to deny the other the right to talk about and proclaim the greatness of the city.

We'll begin our coverage with the gospel on the ground, because without an understanding of the ground and the pull of spiritual gravity toward it, you just might spin off through the air and into outer space.

PART ONE

The Gospel on the Ground

1

God

The work of God in the cross of Christ strikes us as awe-inspiring only after we have first been awed by the glory of God. Therefore, if we're going to talk about the scope of the cross, we need to first talk about who God is. What is he like? How big is he? How deep and wide is his power? The cross provides our access to relate to God, but we must always relate to him in light of who he is, not just who we think or hope him to be. According to James Stewart, "Behind Calvary is the throne of heaven."[1]

If this is true, the deeper we go into God's glory, the deeper we will find ourselves in the precious work of Christ on the cross, and vice versa. Certainly the angels long to look into the gospel of Christ's atoning work (1 Pet. 1:12), because God's glory is in deep, brilliant display there. The great message that we call the gospel begins, then, not with us, or our need, or even the meeting of that need but with the writer of the news and the sender of its heralds: God himself.

We see this need vividly demonstrated in Romans 11 when, in verses 33–36, we find a great primer on the glory of God. The apostle Paul, empowered by the Holy Spirit, writes:

> Oh, the depth of the riches and wisdom and knowledge of God! How unsearchable are his judgments and how inscrutable his ways! "For who has known the mind of the Lord, or who has been his counselor? Or who has given a gift to him that he might be repaid?" For from him and through him and to him are all things. To him be glory forever. Amen.

Paul is basically quoting a song in this passage, and this particular kind of song is something we call "doxology." (The word *doxology* comes from two Greek words that together essentially mean "words of glory.") If you have some church background, you may have sung something called the Doxology—"Praise God from whom all blessings flow"—in your worship services.

Let me tell you why finding the doxology in this place from this author is so interesting. The apostle Paul is not a man given to poetry. This is not the Paul of Peter, Paul, and Mary. This Paul is an unbelievable intellectual who can confuse us. Even the Bible says that Paul is hard to read. If you go to 2 Peter 3:15–16, for instance, Peter says, "I know you've been reading the letters of Paul. Good luck with that." (That's my paraphrase, of course.) We find all kinds of poetry and songs all over the Bible, the Psalms being the most obvious example, but Paul doesn't usually roll that way. His writing is frequently ecstatic, given to long sentences and the piling on of phrases, but he's not really a singsong kind of guy. So how interesting, then, that all of a sudden at the end of the eleventh chapter of Romans, he busts into this song: "Oh, the depth of the riches and wisdom and knowledge of God!"

What is it about the message of the gospel of Jesus Christ, so epically and intellectually and brilliantly laid out in the letter to the Romans, that would drive Paul to break out in song?

God's Transcendent Creativity

In the first century, when Paul wrote Romans, worshipers would have quoted this bit of verse in the temple to convey God's richness and sovereign ownership: "For every beast of the forest is mine, the cattle on a thousand hills" (Ps. 50:10). This way of framing "riches" made sense in the temple, because temple worshipers came from a society built on farming and ranching.

I was born in Seattle, then I moved to San Francisco, which was followed by a move to Houston. Then God was angry and moved me to Abilene for seven years. I finally ended up in Dallas.

Consequently, I'm a city guy. I don't know a lot about farming and agriculture, but here's what I *do* know: the one who owns the cows drives the farming community. You can't plow up your land without them; you can't fertilize without them. So, in agricultural societies, like those of every biblical period, to say, "A thousand hills and all the cattle on them belong to the Lord" is a way to communicate the all-expansive riches of God.

Today, of course, in the metroplex, cows are something we buy to put on property for which we don't want to pay taxes.[2] So it's possible this kind of language doesn't compute very well with us. Most church folk today don't have the background to really understand the importance of knowing God owns the cattle on a thousand hills. We might throw it on some coffee mugs and T-shirts, but when you come right down to it, Psalm 50:10 is a text modern Christians have to chew on a bit, because we live in a day where we can launch things into space and see light-years away.

Every beast in the forest is his. The cattle on a thousand hills belong to the Lord. This means he owns all the cows. And all the hills. He made them both.

Still, maybe cattle aren't your thing. Vaster still are the riches of God. Deuteronomy 10:14 says this: "Behold, to the LORD your God belong heaven and the heaven of heavens, the earth with all that is in it." Read that a second time and see if you can hear what it's saying. According to the Scriptures, every sky on every planet in every solar system in every corner of the universe belongs to God. He is the owner and creator of them all and sovereign over them all. Nothing that exists belongs to anyone else other than God. As Abraham Kuyper famously said, "There is not a square inch in the whole domain of our human existence over which Christ, who is sovereign over all, does not cry: 'Mine!'"[3]

Assuming we are able to acknowledge this truth, we still must do so on a level deeper than that of mere fact. Here's what I mean: you and I are stymied in our own creativity. We can only create as sub-creators, and even then our best work is merely sub-creation.

The human mind is a phenomenal imaginer, and human hands have proven astonishingly skilled. But we are unable to create raw material.

If you're a writer, you can write only as well as you understand language, diction, grammar, and the general art of writing. If you want to paint a picture, you can paint only as well as you have developed your skill, using whatever paints are available to you, in only the colors and combinations that already exist. (Do you see where I'm going with this?) If you want to build a house, you will be fenced in by whatever your credit line is, whatever equipment you can afford, and whatever raw material is already out there. We are great at creating, but our creation is always dependent. Not so with God.

God creates anything he wants and as much of it as he wants, and he does it all out of *nothing*. He doesn't need raw material. He *makes* raw material. God is not limited like you and I are. We are always limited by what's available and always dependent on outside considerations and constraints. When God created the universe, it's not as if the angels walked up to him and said, "Look, God, there are mountains everywhere. There are planets and goats and ostriches and rocks. You've got to get them out of here; we don't have any room to play kickball," so God said, "Well, where can I store this stuff? I know: *the universe*."

Now we're getting nearer to the impulse that caused Paul to sing, "Oh, the depth of the riches and wisdom and knowledge of God!"

Of his own transcendent and self-sufficient creativity, God said to the heavenly host, "I'm going to create the universe." And of course the heavenly host said, "What's a universe?" And after he filled them in on the new creative space to house new creative works, they said, "That sounds awesome, but what are you going to make it out of?" To that God replied, "I'll make it out of myself saying, 'Universe.'" And the universe was formed. Maybe then he said, "I'm going to make some planets now." And the angels said,

"Planets? What's a planet?" And God said, "Planet," and *Poof!*, the planets appeared.

God's creavity is so rich, so expansive, and so far above us that he simply says, "I want this," and there it is. This is just the tip of the iceberg of the things of God that are beyond us. You and I are caged in by what we can afford, what we can gather, and what's already been created. Maybe you've heard of scientists creating life in a laboratory, but that will never happen. No scientist has ever been able or will ever be able to stare into an empty petri dish and wish the nothing it holds into something. Whatever it is scientists do, they do with raw materials already created.

There is nothing confining God. His creativity is transcendent because his very being is transcendent. Everything that *is* is his, and he can make more of anything he wants out of nothing at all. There is no human category for this kind of richness. It makes Bill Gates a pauper, Rockefeller a beggar, and one of those island-owning sheiks in the Middle East a hobo. I don't know what it makes you and me, but it certainly moves us into the perspective of awe that God deserves. Now we get a glimpse of what would move Paul to sing from his soul, "Oh, the depth of the riches and wisdom and knowledge of God!"

God's Sovereign Knowing

How deep is the wisdom and the knowledge of God? God knows every word in every language in every sentence in every paragraph in every chapter of every book ever written. He knows every fact of history past and future, every bit of truth discovered and undiscovered, and every proof of science known and unknown.

In our age, science and faith have become pitted against each other, like yin and yang, as if there is no overlap, as if we must choose one or the other. The Scriptures don't present truth that way though. God owns it all and is so high above our brightest minds that they seem brain damaged in comparison. In 1 Corinthians 3:18–23 we read:

> Let no one deceive himself. If anyone among you thinks that he
> is wise in this age, let him become a fool that he may become
> wise. For the wisdom of this world is folly with God. For it is
> written, "He catches the wise in their craftiness," and again,
> "The Lord knows the thoughts of the wise, that they are futile."
> So let no one boast in men. For all things are yours, whether Paul
> or Apollos or Cephas or the world or life or death or the present
> or the future—all are yours, and you are Christ's, and Christ is
> God's.

This means that truth is never our enemy, ever. So we should
never freak out about people who claim to have discovered truth.
If it's *true* truth, God owns it and has already accounted for it, and
while nothing that is true ever contradicts God's revealed word
in the Bible, discovered truth sometimes contradicts the words of
Christians. We shouldn't be afraid of this, because God knew it
before anybody else and its discovery is dependent on his sovereignty anyway. The truth is that the truth is *ours*; all truth is our
truth because we are of Christ and Christ is of the sovereign God.

Roll this around in your brain a while, because it is more explo-
sive than its simplicity appears: God knows *everything*. He knows
everything at the macro level. He knows the temperature at which
certain stars burn. He knows the orbital lines of planets. He knows
every mountain in every mountain range on this planet and others.
He knows the depths of every ocean. He knows it all at the macro
level.

But he also knows it all at the micro level. He knows every atom
and every molecule. He knows their positions, their locations, their
functions. He sees and governs every instance of mitosis, which, in
case you've been out of school for a while, is one cell becoming two
cells. We have a God who knows everything at the macro level, but
he also knows everything at the micro level.

In addition to the exhaustive depth of his knowledge is the
exhaustive breadth of his knowledge. God is aware of every event
that has ever occurred and will ever occur, and he knows com-

pletely how each event affects other events that create still more events that roll into other events and so on and so forth *ad infinitum*. From the velocity of every butterfly's flapping wings at every second to the exact amount of magma to the microgram flowing out of every volcano above and under sea level, he spans it all simultaneously and precisely. If a tree falls in the woods when nobody's there, does it make a sound? I don't know. But God does.

He knows it all without any sticky notes or strings on his finger. He is holding all things together, seeing all things and knowing all things, all purely from the reality of his wanting it to be so. This is, at the very least, what it means to be God.

If all of this is true, then why in the world do we, with our nanosecond's worth of existence on the earth, still presume to judge how God operates? Paul's cry, "Oh, the depth of the riches and wisdom and knowledge of God!" holds up (as praiseworthy) the enduring reality of divine mystery. Trying to figure out God is like trying to catch fish in the Pacific Ocean with an inch of dental floss. It is a foolish act predicated on a foolish overestimation of human intellect and ability.

In the 1950s and '60s, rationalism began to erode evangelical scholarship, from academia on down, resulting in a liberal theology that crept into seminaries and churches. As a defensive maneuver, conservatives grabbed hold of the pendulum and swung it all the way over to the right side, wanting to believe they'd got "God" down to a science, his thoughts and ways explainable like mathematics. Romans 11:33 tells us instead that God is incomprehensibly immense, exceedingly expansive, and eternally powerful, and so much so that time and time again our response to many of the things of God ought to be "I don't know." Rather than respond to his incalculable God-ness with our slide rules and flowcharts, we would do better to worship him with reverence and awe. How can God see, know, and do all that he does? I don't know.

In the scope of eternity, our life is a blip. James writes, "For you are a mist that appears for a little time and then vanishes" (James

4:14). This crucial truth is at the root of Paul's awestruck confession in Romans 11:33: "How inscrutable his ways!" How could anyone scrutinize God? On what grounds do we find scrutinizing God a legitimate act? Every time we see anything approaching scrutiny of God in the Scriptures, the response of God is a rebuke with the tone of incredulity. As Job is trying to wrap his arms around all that God is doing through the suffering in his life, God says:

> Who is this that darkens counsel by words without knowledge?
> Dress for action like a man;
>> I will question you, and you make it known to me.
> Where were you when I laid the foundation of the earth?
>> Tell me, if you have understanding. (Job 38:2–4)

In other words, "Who do you think you are?" This is one of the most stunning examples of God putting a questioner in his place. "You think you're so smart? Were you there when I created the world? No? I didn't think so. Know your place, son." And I love this "dress for action like a man" stuff. It's like God is saying, "Oh, how adorable you are! Now put on a cup, dude, because it's about to be big-boy time."

When Paul proclaims the hard but glorious truths related to predestination in Romans 9, he anticipates concerns from his readers about God's fairness, so he writes: "But who are you, O man, to answer back to God? Will what is molded say to its molder, 'Why have you made me like this?'" (Rom. 9:20).

My family once made a trip from Dallas to the San Antonio area for my wife, Lauren's, birthday. On the drive down, my then-four-year-old daughter Audrey piped up from the backseat, "Do you know where you're going?" I felt insulted. Lauren started chuckling. She just laughed, and then she asked, "Well, *do* you?"

I said, "Please, I'm on I-35. You just take it straight down."

Then Audrey announced, "I think you're lost."

I said, "I think you're about to get a spanking." (I'm just kidding.)

The whole thing was kind of comical. Four-year-old Audrey has gotten lost in the house. She really has. And we don't have a big house. This is the girl who freaks out if she ends up outside all by herself. This is a girl who has no sense of direction, who has no idea of which way to head to get anywhere, and she's in the backseat presuming to ask me, "Do you know where you're going? I think you're lost."

I said, "Well, um, you can't spell your name. So, there's that."

Okay, I didn't say that either. But this is kind of what happens every time we presume to put God under the microscope of our scrutiny, our logic, or our preconceptions of what he should be like or what he should do.

"How unsearchable are his judgments and how inscrutable his ways!" is God's way of saying through Paul, "Are you serious? You're going to scrutinize how I govern? Do you know how small you are? Do you know how inadequate you are to even comprehend your *own* life? You can't comprehend and figure out your own shortcomings, your own failures, why you're drawn to sin, and why there are things that master you, yet you'll scrutinize *me*?" We are the four-year-old in the backseat telling Dad he doesn't know where he's going.

God's sovereign knowing is so beyond our control and knowledge that acting like we're his GPS or like he's our personal valet is not just laughable but sinful. In Romans 11:34 God becomes terrifying: "For who has known the mind of the Lord, or who has been his counselor?" The answer is *nobody*.

We find this aspect of God's sovereignty terrifying. More often than not, we want him to have fairy wings and spread fairy dust and shine like a precious little star, dispensing nothing but good times on everyone, like some kind of hybrid of Tinker Bell and Aladdin's Genie. But the God of the Bible, this God of Abraham and Isaac and Jacob, is a pillar of fire and a column of smoke. His glory is blinding. It *undoes* people. It takes people out. "It is a fearful thing to fall into the hands of the living God" (Heb. 10:31).

He is wonderful and absolutely terrifying. The god of evangelicalism may be tame and tired at times, but the God of the Bible is *mighty*. "For who has known the mind of the Lord, or who has been his counselor?"

Now, to some degree, we do have revelation from God, so we do know some of the mind of the Lord. He gave us the Scriptures. He speaks to us in dreams and in visions and in words of knowledge—but in no way that runs contrary to Scripture. The Bible says he speaks to us through creation (Ps. 19:1–2; Rom. 1:20). So God has in some sense revealed himself to you and me, but not so much that we would ever be able to counsel him. He has revealed enough of his character and attributes to save us, or preclude us from excuses for irresponsibility in not being saved, but he has not given us enough information to ever, with even a shred of integrity, second-guess him.

Nobody gets to counsel God. Nobody gets to give God advice. Nobody gets to straighten God's path. No one.

God's Perfect Self-Sufficiency

Paul continues in Romans 11:35: "Or who has given a gift to him that he might be repaid?" If everything is God's, you have nothing to give him that he doesn't already own. This means that you cannot put him into your debt. And this means, alternately, that God owes no man anything. Our very existence has been gifted to us by his grace.

While we lament the apparent injustice of pain and suffering, how often do we forget that every good thing in a fallen world is wholly a gift of God's mercy and grace? We think to question God when bridges fall but not to wonder at his grace that every bridge does not. Every fit of laughter, every delectable morsel of food, and every single smile is the result of his mercy and grace; he owes us none of it.

Now let me tell you why this is so terrifying. If this is true, we have nothing with which to negotiate with him, nothing to bargain with. But it has been my experience that most evangelicals believe Christians are in a bargaining position. We carry an insidious prosperity gospel around in our dark, little, entitled hearts. We come to the throne and say, "I'll do this, and you'll do that. And if I do this for you, then you'll do that for me."

In the end God says, "You keep trying to pay me off with stuff that's already mine." Some of us even try to bargain with our lives. But God says, "Please. I'll take that life if I want it. I'm God."

We presume upon our service. "I'll serve you, God!" we say. But he replies, "I'm not served by human hands as though I need anything (Acts 17:25). What are you going to do, give me something to eat? What are you going to do, paint my house? What are you going to give to me, as if I'm lacking?"

The profitable result in these exchanges is the revealing of idolatry and pride within us. We want to live as though the Christian life is a 50/50 project we undertake with God, like faith is some kind of cosmic vending machine. And we're reinforced in this idolatry by bad preachers, by ministers with no respect for the Scriptures, by talking heads who teach out of emotion instead of texts, who tickle ears with no evident fear of the God who curses bringers of alternative gospels (Gal. 1:8–9). He owes us nothing.

And we have nothing to give to him that he doesn't already own outright.

The customary response to this, of course, is to ask about the place of following God and serving his cause. There is plenty of call for this in the Bible. But the reality is that all God has to do is reveal himself to you, and you'll gladly join the mission in service to his kingdom. He doesn't force the issue; he just has to reveal himself as he is: mighty, wondrous, gracious, loving, and radically saving. No man goes back to saltine crackers when he's had filet mignon.

And even this truth is further revelation of God's grace, because it shows that he doesn't need us; rather, he *wants* us. When we who call ourselves Christians realize how utterly self-sufficient God is all within himself—the three in one—the gift of Christ to us and for us becomes all the more astonishing. And we will want it this way. Because a God who is ultimately most focused on his own glory will be about the business of restoring us, who are all broken images of him. His glory demands it. So we should be thankful for a self-sufficient God whose self-regard is glorious.

God's Glorious Self-Regard

Paul continues in Romans 11:36, proclaiming, "For from him and through him and to him are all things." This is an unequivocal declaration that the ultimate origin of everything that exists and *will* exist can be traced back to the hands of God and no further.

Most of us have been told that God created the universe, created all that exists within the universe, and employed the depth of his omnipotence and omniscience to create this because he desired fellowship with man. Have you heard this line of thinking before? It's a very sweet idea, and it would be a great slogan for a Christian motivational poster if it weren't for what the Bible *actually teaches*, which is that this idea is almost blasphemous. Are we to believe that God—in his infinite perfection—was lonely? And that the response to this loneliness was to create a bunch of glory thieves? Is that the infinite God's solution to this hypothetical imbalance in his relational well-being? This is what many of us have been led to believe. And out of our self-regard, we like to picture that a holy, glorious, splendid God—perfect solely within his Trinitarian awesomeness—wanted to be able to stand in a warm-hued living room, romantic music swelling, and look across at us to say, "You complete me."

No. We were not created as some missing link in God's emotional experience. To think this way makes us the centerpiece of the puzzle of the universe! But we are not that close to center.

There are essentially two ways to view the Scriptures. One way is to view them primarily as a guidebook for our daily living. We have questions. Surely the Bible is a reliable reference book. So we ask, should we drink alcohol? Well, let's find that in the Bible. We ask, should I go see this movie or not? And we look up some texts about not eating meat sacrificed to idols and end up slightly more confused but feeling religious, at least. Suddenly we've turned the Bible into our Magic 8-Ball. Of course, we don't call it that. We call it things like "the road map to life."

Now, does the Bible contain a wealth of wisdom for practical, daily living? Yes, absolutely. Is it going to specifically answer every question you've got? Not by a long shot. And on top of that, answering our practical questions isn't the point of the Bible.

Maybe that makes the hair on the back of your neck stand up. Maybe you should shave your neck. Or, if you're married, maybe you could ask yourself if the Bible told you to marry your spouse. When you were deciding what job to take or school to attend, did you find "Take that job" or "Go to that school" in the Bible? When I got a call from Highland Village First Baptist Church almost a decade ago asking if I was interested in throwing a résumé together and interviewing to be their pastor, and I was thinking and praying about what to do, I didn't find the answer in the Bible.

If I'm trying to figure out what I should do or where I should go, I can find general principles about wisdom and guidance and worship in the Scriptures, but I can't find "Marry Lauren, take the position at The Village, buy a minivan" in the Scriptures.

Here's my point: what if the Bible isn't about us at all? What if *we* aren't the story of God's revelation?

The Bible definitely issues commands for us to obey and makes demands for our submission. But, in the end, reading the Bible as the Daily Manual for My Life is the deficient way of the two basic ways available to us. We can read it as a reference book about us. Or we can see that the Bible is a book about God. To paraphrase Herbert Lockyer, the Bible is *for* us, but it's not *about* us.[4]

From beginning to end, the Scriptures reveal that the foremost desire of God's heart is not our salvation but rather the glory of his own name. God's glory is what drives the universe; it is why everything exists. This world is not present, spinning and sailing in the universe, so that you and I might be saved or lost but so that God might be glorified in his infinite perfections.

This is a revolutionary claim, I know. It jostles our hearts and unsettles us. But that's what we're supposed to do with idols (before they are crushed and melted). We are allergic to the idea that everything exists, including us, not for ourselves but for the glory of God. This is why the Westminster divines began their Confession of Faith with their radical answer to the meaning of life: "The chief end of man is to glorify God and to enjoy him forever." But we may as well say that this is the chief end of *everything*. Still not buying it? According to Scripture:

- For the sake of his name, God did not destroy Israel in the desert (Ezek. 20:5–9).
- God saves men for his name's sake (Ps. 106:8).
- Pharaoh's heart was hardened for the glory of God (Ex. 14:4, 18).
- The beginning of the Israelite monarchy was about the glory of God (1 Sam. 12:19–23).
- Solomon dedicated the temple for the glory of God (1 Kings 8).
- Israel became great and powerful among the nations because God was "making himself a name" (2 Sam. 7:23).
- God did not destroy Israel when it deserved to be destroyed, because he did not want his name blasphemed among the nations (Isa. 48:9–11).
- God decided to destroy the Israelites because they would not lay it in their heart to give glory to his name (Mal. 2:2).
- Jesus's life and ministry was about the glory of God (John 7:18; 17:4).
- The cross of Jesus is about the glory of God (John 12:27–28).
- You and I are saved to the praise of his glorious grace (Eph. 1:3–6).
- The Christian life is about the reflection of the glory of God off of our lives into the universe (Matt. 5:16; 1 Cor. 10:31; 1 Pet. 4:11).

- The second coming is about the consummation of the glory of God (2 Thess. 1:9–10).
- The consummation of all things is that God might be praised (Rev. 21:23).

Are you picking up a theme here?

You might say I'm just prooftexting,[5] but this is just the tip of the iceberg. It's not for nothing that the Reformers championed *soli Deo gloria* (glory to God alone)—the Bible screams it from every hilltop and rooftop and into every crook and crevice! The glory of God is God's vision and his plan for seeing it fulfilled. Habakkuk 2:14 promises that "the earth will be filled with the knowledge of the glory of the LORD as the waters cover the sea." The supremacy of God's glory is everywhere in the Bible because God's plan is for it to be supreme everywhere in the world.

This is the story of the Bible, not you or me. It is God and God alone, God's name and namesake alone. The point of everything is God's glory alone so that to God alone will be the glory. It is God who is deep in riches, God who is deep in wisdom, God who is deep in lovingkindness, and God who is deep in glory. Not us. This is the message of the Bible.

God and God alone stands as supreme. There is no court you could complain to, no appellate court in which to have this reconsidered. In fact, the further into the things of God you press, the clearer this truth becomes. A god on the horizon may be squashed with a squinty eye between your fingertips. The God you press your face against extends to ends you cannot see or fathom. John Piper puts it this way: "The further up you go in the revealed thoughts of God, the clearer you see that God's aim in creating the world was to display the value of his own glory."[6]

The Roots of Worship

Piper adds, "This aim is no other than the endless, ever-increasing joy of his people in that glory."[7] We see this in the Westminster

Confession as well: "The chief end of man is to glorify God," yes, but also "to enjoy him forever."

We can call this enjoyment "worship." Worship is the attributing of ultimate worth to something. When this ultimate worth is attributed to anyone or anything other than the one, true triune God of the universe, it is idolatry. The root of Christian worship, then, is acknowledging, submitting to, and *enjoying* the supremacy of God's glory. In all things.

This means, for instance, that God gives us the gift of sex, and it's a good gift, of course, but he did not give us that gift so that our joy might be complete in the act of sex itself. He gave it so that we might be overwhelmed by the goodness of God to give us such a great gift. Sexuality is not an end in itself, nor is it a means to our glory. It is given to us so that we might worship God. Similarly, God gave us food and wine not so that we could guzzle them down and gorge ourselves or so we *wouldn't* enjoy them, but rather that we would take a bite of good food or a sip of great wine and enjoy him by way of enjoying them. First Timothy 4:4 tells us, "Everything created by God is good, and nothing is to be rejected if it is received with thanksgiving."

Worship, when we see it this way, is larger and more encompassing than singing some songs at a church service a couple of times a week. It is the way of life for those entranced by and passionate for the glory of God. We worship God when, while we partake of his good gifts, something occurs in the deepest parts of our soul that forbids glory terminating on the gift itself or on our enjoyment of it but that runs deeper into and extends out to the Giver.

Apart from understanding God and worshiping him in this way, everything becomes superficial. Everything—from dinner to sex to marriage to kids to work to arts and literature—it's all shallow, all trivial. But when you understand the driving force behind everything, all of a sudden there's an eternal amount of joy at our disposal, because everything we do is enlightened and enlivened by the endless glory of the eternal God.

You don't have to be a religious professional to see evidence that this is true. If I wasn't a pastor and wasn't getting paid to say stuff like this, just purely a student of humanity, I don't believe I could argue with the fact that we all seem to be wired for worship. And I don't think it would be difficult to argue that our worship terminates on the shallow and vacuous.

We have a war going on, and a good portion of the world is in an unbelievable mess of poverty, famine, civic unrest, and violence. And yet if you turn on the news in the United States you will be far more likely to hear about the daily activities of pop stars and actors or how much money an athlete is making and who he's dating than anything meaningful. Surely anyone can see that our worship switch is always set to On, and we're tuned to some ridiculously finite broadcasts. Grown men paint their bodies and surf an incalculable number of websites to follow a sports team—significant emotional energy poured into the physical abilities of children in *a game.* Go to any concert and you'll see people lift their hands spontaneously and clap and close their eyes and be spiritually moved by music. People fish or hike to be in tune with nature. We put posters on our walls, stickers on our cars, ink under our skin, and drugs into our system. We do all of these things and others like them, pouring ourselves automatically and quite naturally into what is decaying. We want to worship something. Worship is an innate response. We are wired for it by God himself.

But something has gone wrong with the wiring.

2

Man

We are a worshiping people. Worship is an innate desire, an instinct and impulse wired into us by God himself. This is a gift from God. But what happens when instead of using that gift of worship from God *for* God, we terminate our worship on the stuff God made? What happens when we attempt to hijack God's story about himself and rewrite it with ourselves at the center?

This is insurrection. It is infernal mutiny. What happens when we argue with God about how God should govern, even daring to threaten that if he doesn't govern the way we want him to, we won't believe in him, won't follow him, and will become his enemy?

The Scriptures always paint the universe as a kind of interactive, living thing. For instance, the book of Isaiah says the mountains and hills sing and the trees clap (55:12). Luke 19:40 talks about stones crying out when we don't. All creation groans (Rom. 8:22). The Bible depicts creation as a sort of cosmic concert of interactive worship. In Jeremiah 2, for example, we see that the creation responds in different ways to us in relation to how we relate to God. When God's people embraced idolatry and "changed their glory for that which does not profit," the Lord commanded: "Be appalled, O heavens, at this; be shocked, be utterly desolate" (Jer. 2:11–12).

Why? The universe shudders in horror that we have this infinitely valuable, infinitely deep, infinitely rich, infinitely wise, infinitely loving God, and instead of pursuing him with steadfast passion and enthralled fury—instead of loving him with all our heart, soul, mind, and strength; instead of attributing to him glory and honor and praise and power and wisdom and strength—we just try to take his toys and run. It is still idolatry to want God for his benefits but not for himself. Why would the universe shudder in horror at this idea? (In the original language, Hebrew, the essential idea is that they're literally terrified that God might snap and rip the universe to shreds.) It shudders because the universe is the theater of God's glory and the Scriptures portray this theater as having the instinct itself that it is there to showcase worship. When we, who have been placed as stewards over God's creation, go rogue and worship not the Creator but the creation, the theater is shaken by this blasphemous treason.

What, though, is God's response to this? The universe cowers in terror, but how does God respond to traitors like you and me?

What happens when the mouse tries to steal the lion's dinner?

The Severity of God

In Romans 11:22 Paul covers God's options this way: "Note then the kindness and the severity of God." God's kindness and his severity aren't always mutually exclusive, but Paul is here referring to those who persevere in the faith and those who don't. Those who persevere do so in God's kindness (and because of it). I think the majority of us can grasp this concept. Something approximating the idea of God's kindness is espoused from pulpits every weekend, and when the idea is biblical, it should be. But we *get* that stuff somewhat readily. Grace, love, forgiveness, healing—these are all kindnesses of God, and they should be heard and meditated on and believed. The kindness of God—the *lovingkindness* of God—is a phenomenal theme running through the entire Bible. But Paul didn't stop there in Romans 11:22. The text commands us to note not only the kindness of God but also his severity. (And, in fact, the extent to which we know the freedom of his kindness is contingent upon the extent to which we have known the awfulness of his severity.)

Paul says to note God's severity. Mark it down. Remember it. Consider it. But we are disobedient. Because God's severity is not as warm and fuzzy as God's kindness, we not only don't study or contemplate it, but we don't even note it. We live in a day and age when, from pre-seminary all the way through seminary, prospective pastors are fed the pabulum of church growth. Then once they hit the playing field of ministry they are fed it more and more. From books to classes to seminars to conferences, the church is absolutely consumed with growing at all costs. Forget whether the members of our churches have any real depth or substance to them; we just want to be able to measure and count the three *B*s: buildings, budgets, and butts in the seat. The Bible does say a few things about churches growing in those ways, but today this has become the prevailing mind-set of ministry in evangelicalism, and it is a biblically perverted, missionally distorted mind-set.

This avoidance of the difficult things of Scripture—of sinfulness and hell and God's notable severity—is idolatrous and cowardly. If a man or a woman who teaches the Scriptures is afraid to explain to you the severity of God, they have betrayed you, and they love their ego more than they love you. In the same way that it is not loving or kind not to coach your children on the dangers of the street and the dangers of the swimming pool, so it is not loving not to warn men and women about the severity of God.[1]

When you couple this avoidance with some of the modernist theology that has Jesus floating around like a mystical Ghandi, never angry at anybody, a dispenser of bumper-sticker platitudes and discount fortune cookies, you've got the perfect storm of those who have no awe, no respect, and no real worship for the God of the universe.

Failing to note the severity of God is attempted theft of all he's due. To discount, disguise, or disbelieve what God does in response to the falling short of his glory is, in itself, falling short of his glory. So let's note God's severity. John the Baptist announces:

> I baptize you with water for repentance, but he who is coming after me is mightier than I, whose sandals I am not worthy to carry. He will baptize you with the Holy Spirit and with fire. His winnowing fork is in his hand, and he will clear his threshing floor and gather his wheat into the barn, but the chaff he will burn with unquenchable fire. (Matt. 3:11–12)

We get the impression from the Old Testament that the universe is God's threshing floor. John is warning his hearers that Jesus is going to get to work on the universe, and he's going to gather his wheat into the barn. But the chaff he will burn in unquenchable fire. This is the purpose of Jesus's arrival. (Note in this passage both the kindness and the severity of God.)

The word *Gehenna* is used by Jesus twelve times in the four Gospels. God's first response to the belittlement of his name is this Greek word *Gehenna,* which we would translate "hell." The interesting thing about the word *Gehenna* is that it is a reference to a ravine in the south side of Jerusalem where, about a hundred years before Jesus was born, there were these really odd kind of Blair-Witch–like murders going on. The Jews began to view this area as cursed. It basically became a trash heap or a dumping ground for Jerusalem. When the pile got too big, they just set the whole thing on fire. Can you picture this? The word *Gehenna* conjures up a very vivid image: a stinking, smoldering place of destruction and neglect.

When Jesus uses the word *Gehenna,* he's saying, "It's like this ravine, the valley of Haman; this is what I'm talking to you about." The image to hold in our mind is putrid and repulsive; it is dead and deadly; it is smoldering when not blazing. It is utterly desolate, spiritually dark, and endlessly oppressive, and it is the established picture even in these extremes of the slightest falling short of God's glory.

I have to begin this chapter on the place of man in God's "gospel on the ground" with the information about hell and wrath, because, remember, the Bible is a story principally about God, not man. So, to be faithful to the supremacy of God's glory, I must be upfront about how he responds to attempted glory theft. I must note the severity of God.

God's responses of kindness and severity both come from his perfect and holy self-sufficiency, and they are both extended justly to his creation, but the chief difference between them—and the reason we don't talk about it as much—is that only severity is deserved.

The Fall of Man and the Glory of God

The grace of God by definition is unearned. You can't deserve it. That's kind of the point. "Otherwise," Paul says, "grace would no longer be grace" (Rom. 11:6). Grace is a free gift given to someone who has not earned it and cannot earn it.

But we work so hard. We are awesome people. Surely we deserve something! Yes, absolutely. What we deserve is called "the wrath of God" (expressed in the sentence of eternal death in hell). If you went to Sunday school you probably have heard the following Bible verse, but if you didn't, this is the most succinct summation of mankind's just desserts: "For the wages of sin is death" (Rom. 6:23).

All sin, then, is deserving of the severity of God, and no one is exempt from this. I'll throw the other Sunday school verse at you: "For all have sinned and fall short of the glory of God" (Rom. 3:23). All of us have sinned, and, furthermore, we sin because we're all sinners, and all sinners fall short of God's glory and therefore deserve the eternal severity of God.[2]

"Severity, sure," we may think. "But this *Gehenna* thing? Come on!"

Now, let me tell you why this is such a big deal. According to the Scriptures, everything good and perfect is a gift from God almighty, which means that everything that brings comfort, joy, pleasure, and peace are all gifts from the Father of lights (James 1:17). So hell, when all is said and done, is the absence of God's goodness and blessedness. Therefore, hell is the absence of anything we can think of that's good, right, comforting, joyous, happy, and peaceful. It's a pretty terrifying place. Jesus says that it's a place of gnashing of teeth (Matt. 8:12). He says it's a place where the worm does not die (Mark 9:48). Probably the most hardcore description we find is in Revelation 14:11, which reads, "And the smoke of their torment goes up forever and ever." It doesn't get any more brutal than that.

The point is that if we are going to orient around anything less than God—even things that look happy and shiny and pretty, even things that God himself gives us to enjoy—or slip in even a moment's worship of something other than God, we are declaring our preference for the absence of God. This is called pride, and even a sliver of it deserves its end result: the place where God *isn't*. And let's be honest: nobody has just a sliver of pride.

What's the general response of most sensitive people to the idea of hell? Here's the primary and most popular response: "How can a loving, just God create and fill a place like hell? That's not fair. It's not right. The punishment does not fit the crime. If I tell one lie or steal a pack of gum or say a curse word when I stub my toe, I get eternal torment?"

Am I close? Isn't this where most people's logic lands? "It's not fair."

But to discount the enormity of God's severity, as if we aren't really that bad and really deserve mostly kindness, is to discount the enormity of God's holiness. It is very easy, in this trajectory of logic, to switch things up, completely disregard the Scriptures and the teachings of Jesus, and move into the idea that it's we who are good, and God who is fallen.

"God is love," the thwarters of God's severity say. Of course he is, but the Bible that tells us that is the same Bible that prescribes eternal punishment to the rejecters of his love.

Further, if, as we established in chapter 1, God is most concerned about his name's sake, then hell ultimately exists because of the belittlement of God's name, and, therefore, our response to the biblical reality of hell cannot, for our own safety, be the further belittlement of God's name. Are you tracking with that? Someone who says hell cannot be real, or we can't all deserve it even if it is real, because God is love is saying that the name and the renown and the glory of Christ aren't that big of a deal. Is this the approach we want to take, that hell for eternity is the *wrong* punishment for our belittlement of the glory of God? If so, in essence we say, "The punishment doesn't fit the crime because the crime isn't that big of a deal." Is this justifiable logic? No, it's just a slight case of refusal to be satisfied with the all-sufficiency of the God of the universe.

Do you see that we just ran full circle? Many evangelicals tend to land in this place of God-belittlement and self-justification. "Oh, he wouldn't do such a thing." Well, what about over and over again where he says that he does? Some who don't know the Jesus of the Scriptures at all say that severity and wrath—hell—don't seem like Jesus at all. The Scriptures say that there's a way that seems right to a man, but in the end it kills him (Prov. 14:12).

The correct response to the severity of God, then, is not to dismiss, deny, or denigrate it but rather to repent of our self-regard and throw ourselves back into his glorious self-regard, wondering, "How big and mighty and infinite and glorious is God, that this is the just response for the belittlement of his name?" John Piper helps us again when he says, "The horror of hell is an echo of the infinite worth of God's glory."[3]

The Place of God's Justifiable Wrath

How horrible is this echo? Let's take a look at Matthew 18:8–9:

> And if your hand or your foot causes you to sin, cut it off and throw it away. It is better for you to enter life crippled or lame than with two hands or two feet to be thrown into the eternal fire. And if your eye causes you to sin, tear it out and throw it away. It

> is better for you to enter life with one eye than with two eyes to
> be thrown into the hell of fire.

This passage, by the way, doesn't just give us the comparative negative of hell, but it translates really well into a theology of suffering. With these words of Jesus in mind, I can now know that it is better never to hold my children, it is better never to run my fingers through my wife's hair, it is better not to be able to brush my own teeth, it is better never to be able to drive a car, it is better to be paralyzed and never feel anything from the neck down, and it is better to have stage III anaplastic oligodendroglioma than to find myself outside the kingdom of God.

It is better never to see the sunset or the sunrise, never see the stars in the sky, never to see my daughter in her little dress-up clothes, never to see my son throw a ball—it is better never to have seen those things than to have seen those things and yet end up outside the kingdom of God. How *horrible* hell must be.

What becomes of those committed to the belittlement of God's name?

> Then he will say to those on his left, "Depart from me, you
> cursed, into the eternal fire prepared for the devil and his angels.
> For I was hungry and you gave me no food, I was thirsty and you
> gave me no drink, I was a stranger and you did not welcome me,
> naked and you did not clothe me, sick and in prison and you did
> not visit me." Then they also will answer, saying, "Lord, when
> did we see you hungry or thirsty or a stranger or naked or sick
> or in prison, and did not minister to you?" Then he will answer
> them, saying, "Truly, I say to you, as you did not do it to one
> of the least of these, you did not do it to me." And these will go
> away into eternal punishment, but the righteous into eternal life.
> (Matt. 25:41–46)

The gist of this vital information serves to remind us that all that we have and all that we are and all that we possess was given to us by God, through God, and for the glory of God. When we act like we own these things, like they were given to us *by* ourselves for the glory of ourselves, we belittle the name of God. The universe isn't Burger King; we don't get to have everything made our way. So the weight of Matthew 25:41–46 is not, "You had better feed the poor." The weight of this text is that you have been given much by God to steward in order to be a blessing and primarily a reflection of his glory. Food and drink and clothing are given to us not chiefly for our benefit but for God's glory, and we must find our greater benefit there. That's the gist. But the horrifying implication is that to seek our benefit outside God's glory demands the response of eternal fire.

The bottom line is that to seek our glory is to seek our damnation. In Luke 12:4–5 Jesus issues a somber warning:

> I tell you, my friends, do not fear those who kill the body, and after that have nothing more that they can do. But I will warn you whom to fear: fear him who, after he has killed, has authority to cast into hell. Yes, I tell you, fear him!

This is Jesus's way of saying, "Seriously? You're afraid of what people think of you more than you're afraid of me? You're afraid of what people can do to you rather than what I can do to you? You're more afraid of how people might perceive you than how I perceive you? Are you serious? Listen, the worst they can do is kill you."

This is the gospel's way of asking, "Are you seriously afraid of a kitten and not a lion?" Most of us have a natural and good instinctual fear of physical harm; this keeps stable people from becoming suicidal. So it's not about not caring about whether we live or die *really*. The comparison Jesus is making here is to say that it makes no sense to run up a tree afraid of a kitten while walking up to a lion and slapping it in the face. Will we fear man while flouting God? The reward for that is eternal punishment, which is infinitely more fearful than anything man could whip up.

What does this eternal punishment look like? One of our clearest pictures comes from a parable found in Luke 16:19–26. Jesus relates this story to his hearers:

> There was a rich man who was clothed in purple and fine linen and who feasted sumptuously every day. And at his gate was laid a poor man named Lazarus, covered with sores, who desired to be fed with what fell from the rich man's table. Moreover, even the dogs came and licked his sores. The poor man died and was carried by the angels to Abraham's side. The rich man also died and was buried, and in Hades, being in torment, he lifted up his eyes and saw Abraham far off and Lazarus at his side. And he called out, "Father Abraham, have mercy on me, and send Lazarus to dip the end of his finger in water and cool my tongue, for I am in anguish in this flame." But Abraham said, "Child, remember that you in your lifetime received your good things, and Lazarus in like manner bad things; but now he is comforted here, and you are in anguish. And besides all this, between us and you a great chasm has been fixed, in order that those who would pass from here to you may not be able, and none may cross from there to us."

This is a parable, yes, but it tells us a few things about life in the place of eternal separation from God. It is a place of conscious torment. It is a place of fire. It is a place of anguish. And once you're there, there's no getting out. It is eternal.

There is a chasm between us and the presence of God that manifests the withdrawal of God's presence and goodness from the reality of hell.

The Weight of God's Wrath

The chasm between heaven and hell is illustrative of the chasm between God and us. He is glorious; we are not. He is holy; we are not. He is righteous; we are not. And this chasm between God's total perfection and our total depravity deserves the chasm of stinking, smoldering *Gehenna*.

This is good information to know. It is true information, and it's always good to know the truth. But the problem with this information alone is that it is insufficient to keep us out of the chasm. If someone is heading over a cliff, for instance, it makes little sense to hand him a pictorial display of what will happen when he goes over and crashes onto the rocks below.

What I mean is that we can receive this information about God's severity, we can note it, as Paul tells us to do, and we can explore the biblical array of God's wrath, eternal conscious torment of hell, and how we all deserve both of them, but this information is not sufficient for us to praise God. Have you ever watched Court TV and seen the judge slam down the gavel and say, "I sentence you to die by lethal injection," and heard the convicted party go, "Yeah! I love you, Judge!" No, you haven't. We don't see that, because no one who's guilty wants justice; he wants mercy.

Knowledge of and belief in hell—as important as they are—are unable to create worshipers. Yet misunderstanding this reality is historically how the doctrine of hell has been abused and misued by so many men in the name of God. You cannot scare anyone into heaven. Heaven is not a place for those who are afraid of hell; it's a place for those who love God. You can scare people into coming to your church, you can scare people into trying to be good, you can scare people into giving money, you can even scare them into walking down an aisle and praying a certain prayer, but you cannot scare people into loving God. You just can't do it. You can scare them into moral acts of goodness. But that's not salvation. It's not even Christian.

Even if you could scare people into a semblance of Christian religion, they would not be true worshipers, because their fear of God—which is a good thing—would not be shaped by their love for God. They would not be attracted to God so much as repulsed by hell. Is this true worship? Is true worship choosing the lesser of two fears?

No, to highlight only the breadth of the chasm is not to bridge it. So why highlight it at all? Because you can't understand the cross of Christ without understanding the weight of the glory of God and the offense of belittling his name and what the due punishment is for that offense. What Christ did on the cross will not be revelatory in transforming love until we see that the cross is revelatory also in the depth of the offense of sin. Thomas Watson puts it this way: "Till sin be bitter, Christ will not be sweet."[4] God's love—of which so many hell deniers are such cheerleaders—fails to carry the weight of eternal glory when we don't believe it saves us from much.

When I first got saved, I started reading the Bible, and I learned that a lot of evangelicals use texts completely out of context. My favorite is the one they use out of the prophet that says, "I am doing a work in your days that you would not believe if told" (Hab. 1:5). They throw that on T-shirts, and they print up flyers, and they get architects to draft expansion plans, and they get one of those fundraising thermometer displays in the sanctuary. "God's going to do something amazing in our day, and even if I were to tell you, you wouldn't believe it!" But if you read the rest of the book, the amazing thing he's talking about is killing everybody. He's like, "Literally, I'm going to let your enemies kill you, your families, your donkeys, your cattle, and your business, and I'm going to burn the earth that you walked on." And we put that on our coffee cup. "Something amazing's gonna happen!" Keep reading, dummies; it goes poorly.

Another one evangelicals get tunnel vision about is in the call of Isaiah. The call of Isaiah 6 is a horrific and beautiful passage, where God says in verse 8, "Whom shall I send, and who will go for us?" and Isaiah says, "Here am I! Send me." We stop it right there so it will fit on the direct mailer. But do you know what Isaiah's call was? To preach to people who would never believe.

We play with the eternal weight of glory like a child does a Happy Meal toy.

Here's what I'm wondering: where's Psalm 42:1 for us? Where's "As a deer pants for flowing streams, so pants my soul for you, O God"? Where is that man? Where is that woman? Where is the man who in Psalm 27:4 says, "One thing have I asked of the LORD, that will I seek after: that I may dwell in the house of the LORD all the days of my life, to gaze upon the beauty of the LORD"? Where is that? Where has it gone? Where is that Romans 8 groaning of the heart for the things of God, both over the fallenness of the world and our own tendency to defame the God we love? Where is that? It seems so far from most of us. It seems like we're indifferent and unmoved by the realities of eternity.

We have to feel the weight of God's severity, because without feeling the weight of his severity, we won't know the weight of his kindness, and we won't be able to worship him and him alone. Worship of him is why we were created.

As I write this, March Madness is going on. It's the greatest sporting event. (I say that because it's also the last athletic venue in which David can still beat Goliath. There's not really another venue like it where a college you've never heard of that has, say, eight hundred people in it can upset superstar powers in the basketball world.) But here's the thing about fallen men and women who love March Madness. All over the country, fans are nervous. I'm not joking. They're nervous in their guts, they want their team to win so badly. They watch the games and yell at their televisions: "No! Yes!" Kids are crying in fear, wives are running for more nachos—it's chaos. It's *madness*. With victory comes elation and surfing a thousand websites to read the same article over and over and over again, and with defeat comes destitution of spirit and days of mourning and moping, angrily arguing on a blog about who really deserved it or an official's botched call.

Every bit of those affections, every bit of that emotion, and every bit of that passion was given to us by God for God. It was not given for basketball.

Where is the nervousness in our guts when we're coming into an assembly of those pursuing God? Where is the elation over the resurrection? Where is the desolation over our sins? Where is it? Well, it's on basketball. It's on football. It's on romance. It's on tweeting and blogging.

Are you really going to believe we're not worthy of hell?

Thank God for his response to all this blasphemous nonsense: the wrath-absorbing cross of Christ.

3

Christ

So far we have seen that the Scriptures reveal God as sovereign and glorious and tell us that his sovereign plan is to make manifest the supremacy of his glory. We have also seen that the Bible tells us that we fall short of God's glory in our sinfulness, which is made manifest in our predisposition and efforts to worship things and people that are not God. Because God's passion is for his own glory, then, and because he is perfectly righteous, his response to our idolatry is wrath, eternal condemnation administered by him in consigning us to eternal conscious torment in hell.

This is all needful to know. At least the Bible will shoot us straight. But as truthful and enlightening as it is, the reality of our fallen nature makes this the bad news.

The problem is that, as we have demonstrated, there is a chasm between God and us, and the problem compounding that problem is that not only does our sinfulness cause this chasm, but our sinfulness prevents us from being able to bridge the chasm ourselves. The same law of God that diagnoses our depravity cannot cure it. We are not just down; we are out. There is no pulling ourselves up by our bootstraps in this situation. We have dug ourselves into a grave too deep to climb out. We need radical intervention.

Enter grace.

Note the kindness of God. He loves his children and is therefore patient with them, wanting them all to come to repentance. We deserve his wrath, and even though we persist throughout our lives in foolishly demanding what we think we are due, he refuses to give us what we deserve.

Yet God's innate righteousness demands justice. He cannot let guilt go unpunished. "The wages of sin is death," Romans 6:23 reminds us. Let's throw Hebrews 9:22 in there for good measure: "Without the shedding of blood there is no forgiveness of sins." A blood debt is owed. We have fallen short of the glory of God, and this shortfall must be justified if God is to manifest his sovereign justice.

The place the gospel holds out for us is where God's kindness and his severity meet.[1] This place is called the cross, and it is where grace and wrath intersect. It is at this place of shame and victory that God, in the form of the man Jesus of Nazareth, the long-expected Messiah, offered in his death the blood atonement necessary to satisfy God's justice and secure our salvation.

God's Wrath in Christ's Cross

Jesus, the night before he died, gathered his disciples together for what we call the Last Supper, and he picked up a glass of red wine and said, "This cup that is poured out for you is the new covenant in my blood" (Luke 22:20). Now, if you know anything about the cultural and religious context of the biblical peoples, you know that kind of statement would have sounded unbelievably blasphemous to a first-century Jew. By Jewish law, you weren't even supposed to touch blood. Jesus was not offering up animal blood to handle but his own blood to drink. "This is the blood of the new covenant. Let's drink it up."

I picture confused faces around that Communion table.

So Jesus says, "Okay, let me *show* you."

They leave and proceed to the garden of Gethsemane. Jesus takes three of his disciples and basically says, "Will you guys pray with me? I am overwhelmed to the point of death" (Mark 14:32–34).

Jesus the Messiah, the Son of God in the flesh, is overcome with a desperate sadness! He separates a bit from his dozing friends, falls on his face, and pleads with God, "Father, if you are willing, remove this cup from me" (Luke 22:42), while knowing fully that there is no other way.

A mob led by Judas Iscariot approaches Jesus. Judas walks right up to the face of the man he has called his master, and kisses him on the cheek. Jesus says, "Would you betray the Son of Man with a kiss?" (Luke 22:48).

This story is deeper than just its narrative. It is historical, yes. It actually happened. But there is something spiritually illustrative there of the worship problem in our hearts. The cross of Christ is the response of God to men for belittling his name. The cross of Christ exists because mankind—loved by God, created by God, set in motion by God—betrayed God and prefers his stuff to him. Judas Iscariot, who had walked with Jesus, witnessed the miracles, and wondered at the power of God, kisses Jesus's face in brazen betrayal. In this one little picture, we have the symbol of what's wrong with the universe.

Peter, who had been rebuked only twice in the last hour and a half, decides that he needs another rebuke, so he pulls out his sword and tries to fight the high priest's guards. (Peter's an interesting dude. He unsheathes his sword and takes on the enemy at one moment, but three hours later he doesn't want to fight at all.) He cuts the guard's ear off, but Jesus picks it up, sticks it back on the guy's head, and says, "This is *not* how it's going down. No one's taking my life, Peter. I'm giving it freely."

Jesus is arrested. (Keep in mind that the guard who got healed by Jesus still arrested him. Is that not also illustrative?) Jesus endures six trials; three of the six were illegal according to Jewish law. They beat him severely at each trial. The Scriptures say that they pulled the beard out of his face (Isa. 50:6). They spit on him, and they mock him. They blindfolded him and slapped him and then said, "Prophesy! Who slapped you? Which one of us was the one that slapped you?" (see Luke 22:64). They push a crown of thorns down on his head, and they give him a staff and put a purple robe on him, sarcastically calling, "Hail, King of the Jews" (Mark 15:18). They take the staff from him and beat him with it.

Then Pilate, who wants no part of this, thinks that he can shame Jesus and beat him severely enough that the Jews will let him go. So Christ is beaten until he's a mangled, bloody mess. Do they let him go? The crowd, who five days earlier had shouted "Hosanna! Hosanna!" and laid down palm leaves as Jesus rode into town, now screams, "Crucify him!" (Mark 15:14).

Crucifixion was a work of perverse and grotesque art. As a work of torture unto death, it had been refined and perfected by the Romans over a long period of time. The Romans ruled the world, and in order to rule the world at that time, one needed to wield a lot of fear. So they took this already ancient form of execution and worked to upgrade it,[2] thinking, "If we can slaughter men and women wholesale over an extended period of time in a way that's so horrific that no one would betray us for fear of having this happen, that would be ideal."

They basically beat you and hung you in such a way that, over a slow period of time, your lungs filled with blood until you drowned in your own fluids.

In addition, they appeared to reason that the act of death wasn't enough. They wanted to incorporate humiliation, to heap shame on the agony. Those condemned to crucifixion would first be stripped and put on public display so every lowlife imaginable could taunt them, accuse them, and spit at them. The Romans figured if they could make a spectacle of the condemnation, the deterrent to rebellion would be stronger than execution alone.

God in the flesh was exposed to all of this. They took Jesus then and nailed his hands and feet to a cross. And in the most brutal irony of all ironies, the esteemed high priest was mocking him, the one who wrote the law itself. The one appointed to offer sacrifices for blood atonement was despising the Lamb of God. Did they know that for centuries of the sacrificial system they'd been rehearsing the slaughter of the Messiah?

Jesus the king is being murdered. The sky goes dark in the middle of his crucifixion. A lot of people say that this was indicative

56

of God turning his back on Jesus. The problem with that is what the Bible actually says. Go read Psalm 22. God does not turn his back on Jesus, ever. (By the way: all the sins of the world? God was aware of them before they happened, so it wasn't as if this took God by surprise. Sin is not more powerful than God; it's not radiation to him. God sees everything.)

When the darkness falls, one of the Roman soldiers says, "Uh-oh, maybe he *was* the son of God" (see Mark 15:39). Jesus utters, "It is finished" (John 19:30). The earth shakes and the veil in the temple tears top to bottom. All of this is God's response to the belittlement of his name in the universe. In Acts 2:22–23 we read:

> Men of Israel, hear these words: Jesus of Nazareth, a man attested to you by God with mighty works and wonders and signs that God did through him in your midst, as you yourselves know—this Jesus, delivered up according to the definite plan and foreknowledge of God, you crucified and killed by the hands of lawless men.

The cross of Jesus Christ was not some surprise, not some plan B for God, but rather the plan known about within the Godhead since the beginning. God's response to the belittlement of his name, from the beginning of time, has been the sacrifice of Jesus Christ on a Roman cross.

Acts 4:27 tells us, "For truly in this city there were gathered together against your holy servant Jesus, whom you anointed, both Herod and Pontius Pilate, along with the Gentiles and the peoples of Israel . . ." Now, for the record, that's everyone in the world.

It would be like me saying, "You Americans and all other peoples of earth." This is everyone. Everyone involved in the crucifixion has just been named here. But look at how it continues in verse 28: ". . . to do whatever your hand and your plan had predestined to take place." Whose hand and whose plan? God's plan.

The cross of Christ was God's idea. The death of Jesus was

God's idea. From that first day, when God and Jesus and the Holy Spirit, in perfect unity, said, "Let us make man in our image" (Gen. 1:26), the cross of Christ cast its shadow across all of eternity. It was the predetermined plan of God. The death of Jesus, the wrath-absorbing cross of Christ, was the plan of God before creation.

The cross now stands as the central tenet of all we believe about salvation.

The Satisfactory Sacrifice

Because I didn't have a lot of church background, I struggled for a long time to understand certain phrases common in the evangelical community. First and foremost is this idea about Jesus being the Lamb of God that takes away the sins of the world (John 1:29).

The suffering, this brutal slaughter of Jesus, stands now as the hallmark and message of our faith, and many people have massive problems with it. Some scholars and writers assert that the problem with assigning the slaughter of Jesus to God's sovereign and atoning work is that it amounts to a kind of divine child abuse. The problem with this view, though, is that it's not like God the Father was whipping God the Son without God the Son obliging. If you'll remember, Jesus says, "No one takes My life from Me. I lay it down" (John 10:18). The critics of a cross-centered atonement challenge the priority of the view of penal substitution (or deny its validity altogether), but this creates the problem of all the bloody sacrifices throughout the Old Testament, which Christ's clearly stands in line with. To deny penal substitution is to say that all that sacrificing was incidental.

There are others who approach the issue from a more visceral place. They want to say the cross is simply too gross. It's too horrific. Certainly not a pleasant topic for polite company. "I saw *The Passion of the Christ*," they might say. "It's pornographic." The bloodiness of the cross makes them too uncomfortable. Instead of thinking that maybe that's part of the point, they want to make something else central to the Christian faith besides the cross of

Christ. In fact, I'm still trying to get over the pastor of one of the largest churches in America saying, some time ago on national television, that, at his church, "I never thought about [using the word *sinners*], but I probably don't."[3] If you don't talk about sin, if you don't talk about blood, if you don't talk about the cross in those ways, then don't talk about the gospel, because the gospel is bloody and horrific.

First Corinthians 1:18 says that "the word of the cross is folly to those who are perishing." This is a dire warning to those who find the cross too silly of a doctrine or who seek to diminish its place in the Christian faith to make their calling sure. Those who see the message of the cross as foolishness are perishing.

If we don't understand the bad news, we will never grasp the good news. The bad news is not just that we don't measure up to the law but that by the works of the law none of us will be justified before God (Gal. 2:16). What alternatives to the cross are there? Be a good man? Be a good woman? Be a good Boy Scout or Girl Scout for Jesus? This is what it boils down to for many in the church: replacing the centrality of the cross with something more appealing, something we think is more weighty. In fact, all across the evangelical landscape, people want to get away from the shame and the blood and the guts and the horrific slaughter of Jesus Christ and focus on something else with the cross out on the margins.

But the reason we do this isn't so much to rectify an imbalance but to idolatrously elevate ourselves. It's like the charismatics who want to make the day of Pentecost central to the Christian faith. Or the Calvinists who want to make TULIP central. Liberals want to make social justice the center. Fundamentalists want to make moral behavior the center. (Their motto is "Do, do, do," but the cross screams out "Done!") All of those things are good things, *biblical* things. But to make any of them the center of the Christian faith, the grounds of our hope, is to disregard the only power of salvation—the message of the cross. We end up like Indiana Jones trying to replace the treasure with a bag of sand. We think it will work, but the whole structure comes crashing down around us. Nothing runs to the center of God's kindness and severity, demonstrating his justice, his love, and his glory all at once, besides his incarnate Son's sacrifice on the scandalous cross.

Now, this idea of the removal of sin was put into place thousands of years before the cross. Moses leads the people of Israel out of the bondage of Egypt and into freedom, and as the law is being delivered and established, the children of Israel discover that the way they will worship their Deliverer is inextricably connected to the way their own forefathers—Abel and Noah and Abraham and Isaac and Jacob—worshiped their Deliverer: blood sacrifices. The sacrificial system was instituted under the established truth that to dwell in God's holy presence requires perfection.

Sin is filthy; therefore, sinners are filthy. God will not allow us to belittle his name by assuming our dirty hands are clean enough for the purity of right standing before him. Consequently, in the Old Testament he kills a lot of people. Sometimes it gets pretty wild. The sons of Aaron try to draw near to him, and he kills them. The Ark of the Covenant starts to fall over and a man grabs it and God kills him. This was because you cannot be sinful and get near God. It doesn't work. God's holiness will incinerate you. (Note his severity.)

God essentially says, "No one can come near me without blood. Somebody's got to pay for all of mankind's belittling my name." Without the shedding of blood, there is no forgiveness, remember (Heb. 9:22). Thus the sacrificial system.

Read the book of Leviticus sometime. Leviticus is basically an outline of all the ways God pronounces the atonement equation: "If you commit this sin, this is what it costs." Maybe two doves, maybe a lamb, maybe a goat, maybe a bull, depending on what your sin is.

And in the tent of meetings and in Jerusalem, blood was always flowing. Blood constantly coursed out of slashed arteries and flowed from the temple. Can you imagine the stench in Jerusalem? Can you imagine hundreds and thousands of people regularly carrying a goat, a lamb, a chicken, or a dove into the place of sacrifice and cutting its throat and draining its blood? A river of blood is flowing out of the temple.

God further says, "Here's what we're going to do. Once a year, we're going to do something called the Day of Atonement. On top of all these other sacrifices, once a year, here's what I want. The high priest, the Levite of the house of Aaron, is going to come before me, and he's going to bring a bull and a ram, and he's going to bloodlet those two for his family and himself." So the high priest comes in, kills the bull, drains its blood, kills the ram, drains all its blood, sets them on fire, and then walks out. He then bathes, puts on new linens, a new turban, and a new tunic, and then he brings two lambs and two goats. He brings in the two goats and walks into the Most Holy Place after they've burned incense, and he confesses sin over one goat, and he takes the blade and he bleeds it. Then he prays over the other goat all the sins of Israel, and then they put that goat on a leash and lead him out into the wilderness. One goat *absorbs* the wrath of God toward sin and is killed. The other goat, the scapegoat, is vanquished into the wilderness, carrying away the sins of Israel.

This in a nutshell is the system the worshipers of God lived in for thousands of years. It was brutal, and it's because God is holy, and we are not. Psalm 24:3–4 reminds us:

> Who shall ascend the hill of the LORD?
>   And who shall stand in his holy place?
> He who has clean hands and a pure heart,
>   who does not lift up his soul to what is false
>   and does not swear deceitfully.

The answer to the question might as well read, "Nobody." But there *is* somebody.

Jesus picks up the cup of God's wrath and says, "The old covenant is fulfilled. Drink this, the blood of the new covenant."

And Jesus becomes the Lamb of God. The blade of God's wrath penetrates the Son and bleeds him, and he absorbs the wrath of God toward mankind. The iniquity of man is placed upon the head of Jesus so that, at his physical death, the iniquity of mankind would be carried away. This is what is meant when John the Baptist proclaims his gospel: "Behold the Lamb of God who takes away the sins of the world."

Jesus has bridged the chasm between man and God with his own flesh and blood. What will we do with this?

4

Response

Jesus puts it simply: "Whoever is not with me is against me, and whoever does not gather with me scatters" (Matt. 12:30). The gospel is such power that it necessitates reaction. Jesus Christ has worked such an outrageous wonder that he demands response, whether hatred or passion. Anyone ambivalent about what Christ has actually done just isn't clear on the facts. To present the gospel, then, is to place a hearer in an untenable position. The heart of the hearer of the gospel *must* move, either toward Christ or away from him. Pastor Chan Kilgore puts it this way: "True gospel preaching always changes the heart. It either awakens it or hardens it."[1]

We certainly see this alternating affection and aversion in the four Gospels, as Jesus and his disciples persevere in their itinerant ministry, declaring forgiveness of sins and the inbreaking of the kingdom of God. Some are drawn; others are repulsed. But nobody hears Jesus and just says, "Eh." In some cases, as in the feeding of the five thousand in John 6, they are drawn by his miracles, then repulsed when he connects the miraculous deeds to the miraculous words of the good news.

Knowing this, we don't need all thirty-six verses of "Just As I Am," a plaintive pleading from the altar, heads bowed, eyes closed, and shaky hands raised to issue a gospel invitation. No, the invitation is bound up in the gospel message itself. The explicit gospel, by virtue of its own gravity, invites belief by demanding it.

We each stand from birth on the precipice between life and

death. Because we are stained with sin from conception, we are rushing headlong into the fires of hell before we can even walk.

Jesus lays his body across the path; there is no ignoring him. If it's headlong into hell we want to go, we have to step over Jesus to get there.

Many Christians desire to say yes to the gospel, but one of our biggest problems is mistaking the gospel for law.

Faith versus Works

Here's the funny thing about the Old Testament: 85 percent of it is God saying, "I'm going to have to kill all of you if you don't quit this." Seriously, 85 percent of it is "I am destroying you" or "I am going to destroy you." Because of this, there's a lot of attempted appeasement going on. A lot of scared Israelites need a lot of sacrificial animals. I have no idea how they stocked that many animals. But in all their scurrying around from slaughter to slaughter, God is not just frustrated with their unrepentance, but with their approach to the sacrificial system that they're trying to leverage. Let me show you what I mean:

> Hear the word of the LORD,
>   you rulers of Sodom!
> Give ear to the teaching of our God,
>   you people of Gomorrah!
> "What to me is the multitude of your sacrifices?
>   says the LORD;
> I have had enough of burnt offerings of rams
>   and the fat of well-fed beasts;
> I do not delight in the blood of bulls,
>   or of lambs, or of goats.
> "When you come to appear before me,
>   who has required of you
>   this trampling of my courts?" (Isa. 1:10–12)

This selection from Isaiah highlights the problem with the sacrificial system, both then and now. God doesn't need sacrifices. God is saying, "I don't need your bulls. I don't want your goats. You're missing the point. I'm trying to communicate to you how disgusting and how horrible and how costly your sin is before me. And instead of feeling the weight of that and actually repenting, you just keep doing what you're doing, all the while bringing me goats and bulls like that's what I really want." They're like the wife beater who brings his wife flowers. She doesn't want his stupid flowers. She wants him to repent; she wants to be honored.

The same thing plays out even to this day. Christ's work demands the response of faith, but we want to make donations. It is astounding how many evangelicals are not doing Christianity at all; they're doing the Levitical priesthood. They're trying to offer God good behavior so he'll like them.

We continue living with unrepentant, faithless hearts, making religious pit stops along the way, even frequently, to keep laying things on the altar, and in the end, the altar's closed. When someone dares to insert the unadulterated gospel into this religious mess, we get discombobulated. We get confused. I'm sure the Israelites were confused over prophecies such as that in Isaiah 1. God commands them to come into his temple courts and make these sacrifices, and then he says, "Who has required of you this trampling my courts?"

They're thinking, "Um, *you* did. You told us to do this."

Their heartless obedience—and *our* heartless obedience—demonstrates the bankruptcy of the sacrificial currency.

I'm a fixer, a type-A personality. I like problem solving. Give me a dry-erase board and some markers and throw the problem out there, and I think, "Let's go; let's fix it!" But I learned early on in my marriage that my wife doesn't really appreciate that. She would be telling me about her day, about some problem or frustration she encountered, and say something like, "And this happened and this happened and this happened," and my response was typically, "Let me show you what your problem is."

Husbands, you know this does not go well. I'm a slow learner, but after all these years of marriage, when she tells me something now, I always say, "Are you saying these things because you want me to hear and empathize or are you asking me for help?" I'm so confident in all kinds of areas in my life, but while listening to my wife, all of a sudden, I'm thinking, "Is this a trap?" And I'm realizing something now. I'm realizing that after years of my asking, "Do you want me to empathize or do you want me to help?" I don't think she's ever said, "I'm asking for your help."

The hard-won lesson I've learned in marriage, something I'm very grateful for knowing now, is that there are some things in my wife's heart and some struggles she faces in life that I cannot fix. It doesn't matter how romantic I am; it doesn't matter how loving I am; it doesn't matter how many flowers I send, or if I write her poetry, or if I clean the kitchen, or if I take the kids and let her go have girl time—I am powerless to fix Lauren. (And she's powerless to fix me.) Doing all those things to minister to her are right and good, but there are things in my girl that I can't fix, things that are between her and the Lord. Just like there are things in me that she can't love me enough to overcome.

But the only way I would ever have learned this is to try, try, try—try to fix her, let her try to fix me, and then watch the escalating conflict that takes place when we try to do that.

What if the sacrificial system was given so that we would learn, no matter how much we gave and how much we worked and how many pricey things we sacrificed, that we still can't fix what is broken?

> By this the Holy Spirit indicates that the way into the holy places is not yet opened as long as the first section is still standing (which is symbolic for the present age). According to this arrangement, gifts and sacrifices are offered that cannot perfect the conscience of the worshiper, but deal only with food and drink and various washings, regulations for the body imposed until the time of reformation. (Heb. 9:8–10)

The author of Hebrews is saying that we can sacrifice all we want, and that we can obey all the regulations we can get our hands on, but in the end, if our heart isn't changed, we're no better off. Answer me this: is the alcoholic free if he doesn't drink on Monday but everything in him wants to and needs to, and he's in agony because he wants to do something he knows he can't? Is that freedom? Of course not.

This is what Jesus emphasizes when he says, "You have heard that it was said to those of old, 'You shall not murder; and whoever murders will be liable to judgment.' But I say to you that everyone who is angry with his brother will be liable to judgment" (Matt. 5:21–22); and, "You have heard that it was said, 'You shall not commit adultery.' But I say to you that everyone who looks at a woman with lustful intent has already committed adultery with her in his heart" (vv. 27–28).

You may be able to control yourself against sleeping with somebody you're not married to, and you may be able to avoid taking someone's life, but if you are a slave to lust and anger, you are not any more free than somebody who can't control his urge to murder.

Acts of sacrifice, in the end, don't do anything. They do not cleanse your conscience, and they do not set your heart on the things of God. The routine sacrificial system, then, was not empowered to or designed to cleanse the Israelites' hearts any more than good works are empowered to or designed to cleanse our own. Even our most rigorous of attempts reveals the hardness of our hearts and the insurmountable brokenness inside them. This whole enterprise is a blessed exercise in frustration, but it is one that points beyond itself. Hebrews 10:1 tells us the law is just the shadow of the good things to come.

Similarly, the shadow of good works ought to proceed from the light of the good news. Our endless, bloody religious sacrifices ought to push us to look to the one sacrifice to rule them all. The gospel of the sacrifice of Christ on the cross, then, is not an invitation to moralism; it is an invitation to real transformation. Our works don't work. "For we hold that one is justified by faith apart from works of the law," Paul writes in Romans 3:28. The only acceptable response to the gospel is nothing less than a heart of faith.

Clay and Ice, Cuts and Scars

The Puritans had a saying: "The same sun that hardens the clay melts the ice."

I was converted to belief in Jesus Christ as savior and Lord over a period of time, so I don't have the testimony of those who say, "I was at a Billy Graham Crusade; I heard the gospel for the first time, and I was all in." Although my justification was secured in a moment, the process of my understanding and acceptance took place over a year-long time of some guys being patient with me and loving me and walking with me. They invited me to church gatherings and spiritual events, and they even allowed me to mock those things. They just patiently explained them to me more fully. I asked a lot of questions that I now know won't be answered this side of heaven, but they let me ask them anyway, and they tried to answer. Sometimes they'd give me books to read. Through that whole year, God began to gather kindling around my life.

You start a fire with small pieces of grass and wood, and once that's caught, you put on bigger sticks, and then you put on bigger sticks, and then you put on even bigger sticks. In those early conversations with my friends Jeff and Jerry and others, God was laying kindling around my heart, and then, three days before my eighteenth birthday, he lit it up. What's funny is that in that moment I no longer needed all my questions answered. It took me a while to catch, but when I did, that's when I was all in.

Before that, though, I needed to know how it all worked; I needed to know how everything fit; I needed to know why God would say such-and-such. But when the Holy Spirit opened up my heart to Christ my savior and God my Father and reconciled me to God, I didn't need those questions answered. Even after my conversion, the residual contention I held out, that some specific complexity has to be solved for this whole thing to be credible, melted away in the light of God's grace and mercy in my life. In May of that decisive year, I was an aggressive agnostic. In June I was converted and began to share the gospel.

I should explain what I mean when I say I shared the gospel. At that time, I knew that if you don't love Jesus, you are going to hell, and therefore you shouldn't drink beer and try to sleep with girls. That was the sum total of my frame of reference; I wasn't theologically built out. But I had an insatiable thirst for the Word of God, so I studied the Bible constantly. Even so, I knew nothing of deep books, deep thinking, and the deep realities of the good news. I just knew that I loved Jesus, that I wanted other people to love Jesus, and that if you didn't love Jesus the way I did, you were going to hell. That was my evangelistic strategy, so I told almost everyone I knew about this fantastic news: "This is what has happened to me. This is what God has done. This is what Jesus has done for *you*!"

In God's mercy, he covered my naivete and honored my sincerity with the powerful gospel in spite of me, and I actually won people to Christ. I began to see a great deal of openness to the good news among my friends. Several came to know the Lord right after I did and began to follow him, love him, and serve him, and they continue to do so to this day. What I learned in those early days is that the proclamation of the glory of God, the might of God, and the majesty of God brought to bear on the sinfulness of man in the atoning work of Jesus Christ actually stirs the hearts of men. And men respond to that stirring. Some are stirred to belief; some are not.

I remember some friends who were stirred not to belief but to interest. "Explain this to me," they'd say. "Help me understand this." But, in the end, those guys were hardened to the gospel, and as time went on, and as they asked more questions, they didn't become more and more open to Christ but more and more closed to him.

This is what the gospel does. This is why the gospel of Jesus is dangerous. When we hear the gospel word, we are opened up to the Word of God. We're subjected to God's Word reading *us*. We sit underneath it, and for the moment of our hearing, it rules us. It does not save all, but all who hear it are put in their place. This is dangerous, because the proclamation of God's Word goes only one way or another in the soul of a man, and one of those ways is the hardening of a man toward the grace of God.

This means, for instance, that nobody can really attend church as though it's a hobby; to do so does not reveal partial belief but hardness. The religious, moralistic, churchgoing evangelical who has no real intention of seeking God and following him has not found some sweet spot between radical devotion and wanton sin; he's found devastation. The moralism that passes for Christian faith today is a devastating hobby if you have no intention of submitting your life fully to God and chasing him in Christ.

It is an amazing thing, but this one message can reach both those who are near and those who are far (Eph. 2:17) and bring one person near and push another farther away. The same sun that hardens the clay melts the ice.

Jesus gives us some insight into this phenomenon in his parable of the sower in Matthew 13:1–8. The sower does not offer a different seed in all his scattering; he apparently doesn't even adjust the way he scatters. He has one seed, and evidently he distributes it indiscriminately. He knows every soil needs this one seed to grow what only this one seed produces. The different responses to the seed are contingent upon the receptivity of the soil. The seed finds purchase in soft soil but does not in hard soil.

I think of the way the Word of God, which is "sharper than any two-edged sword" (Heb. 4:12), cuts into the soul of every man and woman. The Word is sharp; there's no doubting that. But some souls it cuts to the quick, breaking open like freshly tilled soil; others it bruises, leaving marks scarred over. This is not because the sword is not sharp enough, or that God cannot cut to the quick any soul he wants. Our softness or hardness is subject to the good pleasure of God (Rom. 9:18). Nevertheless, the effect is such that the sharp word of the gospel cuts some open, and others it scars, further callousing them against its promise of life. There is no one in between.

Response and Responsibility

A lot of Christians love Isaiah 6, and this is because they stop reading before the story is over. Let me show you what I mean:

> In the year that King Uzziah died I saw the Lord sitting upon a throne, high and lifted up; and the train of his robe filled the temple. Above him stood the seraphim. Each had six wings: with two he covered his face, and with two he covered his feet, and with two he flew. And one called to another and said: "Holy, holy, holy is the LORD of hosts; the whole earth is full of his glory!" And the foundations of the thresholds shook at the voice of him who called, and the house was filled with smoke. And I said: "Woe is me! For I am lost; for I am a man of unclean lips, and I dwell in the midst of a people of unclean lips; for my eyes have seen the King, the LORD of hosts!" Then one of the seraphim flew to me, having in his hand a burning coal that he had taken with tongs from the altar. And he touched my mouth and said: "Behold, this has touched your lips; your guilt is taken away, and your sin atoned for." (vv. 1–7)

Evangelicals love this text. It radiates the exaltation of God. It conveys a thrilling *bigness*. Then you have verse 8, which is a definite coffee-cup verse: "And I heard the voice of the Lord saying, 'Whom shall I send, and who will go for us?' Then I said, 'Here am I! Send me.'" We absolutely love Isaiah 6:8. We romanticize it. So when we hear a sermon on missions, and the preacher has moved into leading a "Let's do something good for the Lord" cheer, we feel the gravitational pull toward Isaiah 6:8: "Here am I! Send me."

It sounds gutsy, masculine. We can hear *Braveheart*'s guttural yawp in there. "Let's do it! Let's take it! Let's go get 'em!"

We are as zealous about Isaiah 6:8 as we are oblivious of Isaiah 6:9. There is a roadblock waiting for us there: "And he said, 'Go, and say to this people: "Keep on hearing, but do not understand; keep on seeing, but do not perceive.""" Do you see what is happening here? God says, "Here's your ministry, Isaiah. Go tell them, 'Keep on hearing but do not hear.'"

Experientially, we know exactly what this means. We have all at some point said the right words to people who simply are not hearing them. The phrase "It's like talking to a brick wall" is common for a reason. One of my frustrations living in the Bible Belt is that the gospel and its ancillary truths have been so divorced from actual living that a lot of beautiful theology has become cliché. There is a sentimentalization of the faith that occurs when you sanitize the gospel of Christ crucified or sift it from the substance of the Christian religion. The result is a malleable Jesus, a tame Jesus. The result is, as Michael Spencer says, "a spirituality that has Jesus on the cover but not in the book."[2] When we dilute or ditch the gospel, we end up with an evangelicalism featuring special appearances by Jesus but the denial of his power (2 Tim. 3:5).

I meet a lot of people swimming neck deep in Christian culture who have been inoculated to Jesus Christ. They have just enough of him not to want all of him. When that happens, what you have are people who have been conformed to a pattern of religious behavior but not transformed by the Holy Spirit of God. This explains why we see a lot of people who know objective spiritual truths but in the end have failed to apply them in such a way that their lives demonstrate real change. They're hearing, but they're *not* hearing.

A really vivid way we see this occur at The Village is in response to what the staff jokingly calls my "State of the Union" addresses, in which I say to the congregation, "Hey, quit coming here. If you're not serious, if you don't want to plug in, if you don't want to do life here, if you don't want to belong, if you're an ecclesiological buffet kind of guy, eat somewhere else." And then people who are doing all of those things will sit there in the crowd and say, "Yeah! Get 'em. It's about time someone said this." I'm thinking, "I'm talking to you! *You're* who I'm talking to." It makes me want to pull my hair out. They hear the words coming out of my mouth, but they're not listening.

God commands Isaiah, "Tell them to keep on seeing, but not to perceive."

Have you ever come across someone who absolutely knows his life is a mess but cannot put the dots together to see that he's a part of the issue? If you run into someone with a victim's mentality, someone who is constantly leaving carnage in her wake, someone who has a new group of friends every twelve to fifteen months, someone who has story after story after story about how this person betrayed him and another person did him wrong, but he has no ability to see or comprehend that he is the common denominator, you've run into someone who can see but can't perceive. Such people know their life is a mess, but they can't figure out, "Hmm, I seem to be the major malfunction here." As it relates to spiritual matters, this seems to apply to all mankind.

God continues in Isaiah 6:10:

> Make the heart of this people dull,
>   and their ears heavy,
>   and blind their eyes;
> lest they see with their eyes,
>   and hear with their ears,
> and understand with their hearts,
>   and turn and be healed.

Now, nobody wants this ministry. Can you imagine this want-ad?

> Now hiring: Pastor. Must make hearts dull. Those seeking fruitful ministry need not apply.

73

For all the ambition that I've seen in young preachers, not a single one of them has said, "I want to be faithful to the Word of God and have no one respond to it." So Isaiah does what any of us would do, and he asks about it:

> "How long, O Lord?"
> And he said:
> "Until cities lie waste
>   without inhabitant,
> and houses without people,
>   and the land is a desolate waste,
> and the LORD removes people far away,
>   and the forsaken places are many in the midst of the land.
> And though a tenth remain in it,
>   it will be burned again,
> like a terebinth or an oak,
>   whose stump remains
>   when it is felled."
> The holy seed is its stump. (vv. 11–13)

God's response to Isaiah is simply this: "I'm going to gather the remnant. I'm going to gather the genuine believers. I'm going to work this thing over until all that is left are those who really love me, trust me, and seek me." Isaiah, then, is not called to be fruitful but simply to be faithful. And, in fact, he's told he will not be fruitful. The priority God charges him with is not success but integrity. He is sent to proclaim a word to people who in the end can see but not perceive, who can hear but can't hear.

Let us allow the implications of this for Christian ministry settle into our minds. Let's steep in this text; let's wrestle with it. Let all of us Christians do this, but we in church leadership especially need to come to terms with what exactly happened there in the temple.

God's commissioning of Isaiah is a torpedo into the way ministry is appraised in the church today. God is saying, "Isaiah, you're going to proclaim faithfully, but they're going to reject continually. And I'm at work *in that*." Now, if Isaiah was a minister within today's evangelicalism, he'd be considered an utter failure. Jeremiah would be an utter failure. Moses didn't get to enter the Promised Land. John the Baptist didn't get to see the ministry of Jesus. On and on we could go. We would not view the ministry of these men as successful.

One of the things we don't preach well is that ministry that looks fruitless is constantly happening in the Scriptures. We don't do conferences on that. There aren't too many books written about how you can toil away all your life and be unbelievably faithful to God and see little fruit this side of heaven. And yet God sees things differently. We always have to be a little bit wary of the idea that numeric growth and enthusiastic response are always signs of success. The Bible isn't going to support that. Faithfulness is success; obedience is success.

What we learn about God's call to Isaiah provides a strange sense of freedom. A hearer's response is not our responsibility; our responsibility is to be faithful to God's call and the message of the gospel. No, a hearer's response is his or her responsibility. But one of the mistakes we can make in our focusing on individual response in the gospel on the ground is to lose sight of God's sovereign working behind our words and actions and our hearer's response. Receptivity and rejection are ultimately dependent upon God's will, not ours.[3] Paul reminds us, "[God] says to Moses, 'I will have mercy on whom I have mercy, and I will have compassion on whom I have compassion.' So then it depends not on human will or exertion, but on God, who has mercy" (Rom. 9:15–16). From the ground, we say what we choose to say and hear what we choose to hear. From the air, our saying is clearly empowered— "No one can say 'Jesus is Lord' except in the Holy Spirit" (1 Cor. 12:3)—and our hearing is clearly God-contingent—"having the eyes of your hearts enlightened" (Eph. 1:18).

You can find a whole bunch of verses about God's moving and gathering large groups of people, which means if there's numeric growth and much enthusiasm, we can't say that it's not a work of God or that God isn't moving. I'm just saying that I guarantee you there's some old dude in some town that most of us have never heard of faithfully preaching to nine people every week, and when we get to glory, we'll be awed at his house. We'll be awed at the reward God has for him. In the end, we have this idea being uncovered in Isaiah that God hardens hearts, that people hear the gospel *successfully* proclaimed and end up not loving God but hardened toward the things of God.

I know some people think, "Well that's Old Testament, and God was really angry then. But Jesus is a lot nicer than God." (Should we set aside the fact that Jesus *is* God?) But God's sovereignty over the hardened response of hearers is well laid out in the New Testament too. Let's return to the parable of the sower. In Matthew 13 Jesus tells us about the guy who casts the seeds. Some seeds land on the path, some land among the thorns, some land on shallow ground, and some land on good soil. After Jesus tells the parable, his disciples approach him confused because nobody can understand it. They ask him, "Why do you do this? Why do you tell these stories? Nobody knows what you're talking about." Here is Jesus's response: "To you it has been given to know the secrets of the kingdom of heaven, but to them it has not been given" (Matt. 13:11).

Now if we just stopped there and stared at this verse, we could find real joy for a long time. Right now, there are millions and millions of people who have no idea about the kingdom of heaven. But not you. You know the secret. They have no idea about the kingdom, no idea about God's grace, no idea of God's mercy. But not you. You know. You get to worship him, you get to walk with him, and you get to hear from him. Jesus tells his disciples, "It hasn't been given to them. It has been given to you." And he continues:

> For to the one who has, more will be given, and he will have an abundance, but from the one who has not, even what he has will be taken away. This is why I speak to them in parables, because seeing they do not see, and hearing they do not hear, nor do

they understand. Indeed, in their case the prophecy of Isaiah is fulfilled that says:

> "You will indeed hear but never understand,
>   and you will indeed see but never perceive.
> For this people's heart has grown dull,
>   and with their ears they can barely hear,
>   and their eyes they have closed,
> lest they should see with their eyes
>   and hear with their ears
> and understand with their heart
>   and turn, and I would heal them."

But blessed are your eyes, for they see, and your ears, for they hear. For truly, I say to you, many prophets and righteous people longed to see what you see, and did not see it, and to hear what you hear, and did not hear it. (Matt. 13:12–17)

So on both sides of the covenant—old and new—we see that God is in control. His sovereignty is not diminished or thwarted. The hearer of the gospel is responsible for his response, but God is responsible for his ability to do so. The preacher of the gospel is responsible for his proclamation, but God is responsible for the transforming power.

The gospel message goes out, and while some hearers respond with faith in Christ, some people simply can't hear.

The Unadjusted Gospel Is the Empowered Gospel

It is all of grace that some *do* hear. At the close of chapter 3 we asked, "What will we do with Christ's substitutionary work?" The answer is, "Whatever the Spirit allows us to." Blessed are the eyes that see and the ears that hear because the Spirit of God has opened them to do so. The power in the gospel is not the dynamic presentation of the preacher or the winsomeness of the witness, although the Spirit does empower and use those things too. The power in the gospel is the Spirit's applying the saving work of Jesus Christ to the heart of a hearer. Charles Spurgeon puts it this way:

You cannot induce them to come; you cannot force them to come by all your thunders, nor can you entice them to come by all your invitations. They *will not* come unto Christ, that they may have life. Until the Spirit draw them, come they neither will, nor can.[4]

In Acts 2 we find the first post-ascension sermon of the Christian church. The apostle Peter addresses the crowd that has witnessed the response of many to the outpouring of the Spirit:

Men of Judea and all who dwell in Jerusalem, let this be known to you, and give ear to my words. For these people are not drunk, as you suppose, since it is only the third hour of the day. But this is what was uttered through the prophet Joel:

"And in the last days it shall be, God declares,
that I will pour out my Spirit on all flesh,
and your sons and your daughters shall prophesy,
     and your young men shall see visions,
     and your old men shall dream dreams;
even on my male servants and female servants
     in those days I will pour out my Spirit, and they shall prophesy.
And I will show wonders in the heavens above
     and signs on the earth below,
     blood, and fire, and vapor of smoke;
the sun shall be turned to darkness
     and the moon to blood,
     before the day of the Lord comes, the great and magnificent day.
And it shall come to pass that everyone who calls upon the name of
     the Lord shall be saved." (Acts 2:14–21)

Peter begins the very first Christian sermon with the majesty of God. If there is prophecy, if there is utterance, if there is the miraculous, if there is power, if the sun is darkened, if there is vapor, if there is blood and fire, where does it all start? With God.

God prophesied; God said this would happen, and he brought it about. Peter is basically saying, "All that you understand about the prophets, all that you understand about the miraculous works of God, and all that you understand about how God moves is wrapped up in the Godhead, who saves all who call on him." Look what he says next:

> Men of Israel, hear these words: Jesus of Nazareth, a man attested to you by God with mighty works and wonders and signs that God did through him in your midst, as you yourselves know—this Jesus, delivered up according to the definite plan and foreknowledge of God, you crucified and killed by the hands of lawless men. God raised him up, loosing the pangs of death, because it was not possible for him to be held by it. For David says concerning him,
>
>> "I saw the Lord always before me,
>>> for he is at my right hand that I may not be shaken;
>> therefore my heart was glad, and my tongue rejoiced;
>>> my flesh also will dwell in hope.
>> For you will not abandon my soul to Hades,
>>> or let your Holy One see corruption.
>> You have made known to me the paths of life;
>>> you will make me full of gladness with your presence."
>
> Brothers, I may say to you with confidence about the patriarch David that he both died and was buried, and his tomb is with us to this day. Being therefore a prophet, and knowing that God had sworn with an oath to him that he would set one of his descendants on his throne, he foresaw and spoke about the resurrection of the Christ, that he was not abandoned to Hades, nor did his flesh see corruption. This Jesus God raised up, and of that we all are witnesses. Being therefore exalted at the right hand of God, and having received from the Father the promise of the Holy Spirit, he has poured out this that you yourselves are seeing and hearing. For David did not ascend into the heavens, but he himself says,
>
>> "The Lord said to my Lord,
>> 'sit at my right hand,
>>> until I make your enemies your footstool.'"
>
> Let all the house of Israel therefore know for certain that God has made him both Lord and Christ, this Jesus whom you crucified. (vv. 22–36)

So we have this incredible sermon exulting in the majesty of God, tying God's work in the incarnation of Jesus Christ back to the promises of the Old Testament, specifically to David's promise of an eternal king. But the refrain echoing in this text is, "You crucified him, you killed him, you did this."

This is not a seeker-sensitive sermon. Peter does not shrink back, fearing, "Oh man, this is going to be offensive." He is not thinking, "How can I make this sound cool to the young Jerusalemites that are here? How can I soften this?" He knows that if he tells them they killed Jesus, they're going to get really angry. But he says anyway, "You killed Jesus." Then he says it again. "Oh yeah, this majesty? You killed it."

We are never, ever, ever going to make Christianity so cool that everybody wants it. That is a fool's errand. It is chasing the wind. We can't repaint the faith. It doesn't need our help anyway.

Every effort to remake the Christian faith leads to wickedness. Every effort to adjust the gospel so it appears more appealing, more palatable, is foolishness. This is liberal theology's only play in the playbook. "Let's get rid of the atoning work of Jesus Christ because it's harsh. Let's get rid of hell because it's offensive. Let's save Christianity by changing Christianity." But in the urban context of Acts 2, with people all over the ancient world gathered in Jerusalem, Peter announces, "You killed him. This majestic one true God of the universe—you crucified him." And what happens?

> Now when they heard this they were cut to the heart, and said to Peter and the rest of the apostles, "Brothers, what shall we do?" And Peter said to them, "Repent and be baptized every one of you in the name of Jesus Christ for the forgiveness of your sins, and you will receive the gift of the Holy Spirit. For the promise is for you and for your children and for all who are far off, everyone whom the Lord our God calls to himself." And with many other words he bore witness and continued to exhort them, saying, "Save yourselves from this crooked generation." So those who received his word were baptized, and there were added that day about three thousand souls. (vv. 37–41)

All they did was preach the gospel, and men were cut to the core. They wanted to know, "What do we do in response to this news?" Peter tells them, "You repent and get baptized."

What saved them? Their faith. No action brought about their salvation. They hadn't fed any poor people. Apart from what Peter is saying here, they hadn't been sitting under teaching or going to church each week. They hadn't, in the end, done anything but heard, "God is majestic, and you have sinned, but in Christ you can be reconciled to him," and they were so cut to the heart that they responded with saving faith.

Acts 2 takes us back to the truth that we simply have to tell. God does the opening of hearts.[5] God opens minds. There is such freedom in this! Do you see how that takes weight off the perfection of our presentation? We don't have to be able to explain it absolutely or completely or be able to apologetically defend creationism or argue the falsity of materialism or whatever. I'm not saying we shouldn't pursue those things. I'm saying that in the end it is God who opens up eyes and ears. Our responsibility is to tell them. It is as simple as that.

Some people won't like hearing it. What else is new? This has been true as far back as Genesis. It has always been true that some people do not want to hear this message. But some are going to hear it and be saved. So, relational evangelism? Go for it, as long as it turns into actual evangelism. You hanging out having a beer with your buddy so he can see that Christians are cool is not what we're called to do. You're eventually going to have to open up your mouth and share the gospel. When the pure gospel is shared, people respond.

The spiritual power in the gospel is denied when we augment or adjust the gospel into no gospel at all. When we doubt the message alone is the power of God for salvation, we start adding or subtracting, trusting our own powers of persuasion or presentation. We end up agreeing with God that preaching is foolishness (1 Cor. 1:21) but disagree that it is required anyway. This is a colossal fail. Only the unadjusted gospel is the empowered gospel. And this message of the finished work of Christ's life, death, and resurrection for the forgiveness of sins and the securing of eternal life is carried by the Spirit like a smart bomb into the hearts of those the Spirit has given eyes to see and ears to hear.

Response to the Gospel Is Not the Gospel

One crucial thing that viewing the gospel on the ground helps us do is distinguish between the gospel's content and the gospel's implications. One danger of viewing the gospel in the air is the conflating of the good news with its entailments. As we rightly see the gospel as encompassing God's work, through the culmination of Christ, of restoring all things, we can be tempted to see our good works, whether preaching Scripture or serving meals at a homeless shelter, as God's good news.[6] This is a temptation that honing in on the ground gospel can help us identify and mark out. We need to rightly divide between gospel and response, or we compromise both. D. A. Carson writes:

> The kingdom of God advances by the power of the Spirit through the ministry of the Word. Not for a moment does that mitigate the importance of good deeds and understanding the social entailments of the gospel, but they are entailments *of the gospel*. It is *the gospel* that is preached.[7]

We can exercise this delineation by continuing in Acts 2:

> They devoted themselves to the apostles' teaching and the fellowship, to the breaking of bread and the prayers. And awe came upon every soul, and many wonders and signs were being done through the apostles. And all who believed were together and had all things in common. And they were selling their possessions and belongings and distributing the proceeds to all, as any had need. And day by day, attending the temple together and breaking bread in their homes, they received their food with glad and generous hearts, praising God and having favor with all the

people. And the Lord added to their number day by day those who were being saved. (Acts 2:42–47)

All the things that prompt people to mistakenly say, "This is the gospel," can be found in this passage. What we actually see in Acts 2:42–47 is the beautiful fallout of the proclamation that precedes it. This list tells us the hearers' *response* to the gospel. Why did they start living in community? Because the gospel had made them a people. Why did they begin to share their goods with one another? Because the gospel had made them a people. Why are they now on mission? Because the gospel had made them a people. Why are they seeing signs and wonders? Because the gospel had made them a people. All of these workings are outworkings of the gospel.

If we piggyback the work of the church onto the message of the gospel, we don't enhance the gospel. It is just fine without us; it doesn't need us. Furthermore, doing that results in preaching the church rather than preaching Christ. "For what we proclaim is not ourselves," Paul writes, "but Jesus Christ as Lord, with ourselves as your servants for Jesus' sake" (2 Cor. 4:5).

Believing the news that God is holy, that you are a sinner, and that Christ has reconciled you to God by his life, death, and resurrection is what justifies you. This is our foundation, our root. The things that we read in Acts 2:42–47 are the fruit. They show the building of the home, but they are not the foundation.

If we confuse the gospel with response to the gospel, we will drift from what keeps the gospel on the ground, what makes it clear and personal, and the next thing you know, we will be doing a bunch of different things that actually obscure the gospel, not reveal it. At the end of the day, our hope is not that all the poor on earth will be fed. That's simply not going to happen. I'm not saying we shouldn't feed and rescue the poor; I'm saying that salvation isn't having a full belly or a college education or whatever. Making people comfortable on earth before an eternity in hell is wasteful.

The Response of Faith

Everybody comes out of the womb in rebellion. David says, "Behold, I was brought forth in iniquity, and in sin did my mother conceive me" (Ps. 51:5). David doesn't even get himself out of the birth canal before he thinks, "Sinner!" What are we like apart from Christ? What is our default position from conception? Ephesians 2:1–3 says that we're: (1) dead; (2) world followers; (3) devil worshipers; (4) appetite driven; and (5) children of wrath.

I am not sure it is possible to be worse than this. But the good news is that upon the proclamation of the gospel of Jesus Christ, God raises, rescues, ransoms, reforms, and reconciles. God saves sinners. Does he save all? No, but he saves.

People are going to respond to the gospel every time it is presented. They're going to respond in belief, or their heart is going to become more and more hardened toward God. But no heart can ever be too hard for God. Some hearts will grow harder and harder each day until the day God's mercy blows them up like dynamite. We have seen tons of people at The Village who sat here for years just hearing but not hearing, seeing but not perceiving, and then all of a sudden, at some random worship service or Bible study, the Lord just hijacked them, the way that Paul was apprehended (Phil. 3:12). In that moment of rebirth, all those steps toward hardening get evaporated in fire from heaven.

The gospel is news, not advice or instruction, but it nevertheless demands response. So, if we look at our lives today, a question I think we have to ask ourselves is this: "How am I responding to the good news of Jesus Christ? Am I stirred up toward obedience, or is Jesus becoming cliché to me? Am I becoming inoculated to Jesus, or do I find myself being more and more stirred up to worship him, to let other people know him, to submit my life fully to him?" We have to ask these questions, because everybody responds to the gospel. We must test ourselves to see if we are in the faith (2 Cor. 13:5), because it is faith by which salvation comes. Faith is the only saving response to the gospel.

Every good gift the Father gives—every richness from Christ, every blessing from the Spirit—flows from the gospel and is received through faith.

- We receive righteousness through faith (Rom. 3:22).
- We are justified through faith (Rom. 3:30; Gal. 2:16).
- We stand fast through faith (Rom. 11:20).
- We are sons of God through faith (Gal. 3:26).
- We are indwelled by Christ through faith (Eph. 3:17).
- We are raised with Christ through faith (Col. 2:12).
- We inherit the promises through faith (Heb. 6:12).
- We conquer kingdoms, enforce justice, and stop the mouths of lions through faith (Heb. 11:33).
- We are guarded through faith (1 Pet. 1:5).

We live through faith, and we die through faith. Everything else is garbage. Even works of righteousness, if not done through faith, are works of self-righteousness and therefore filthy rags. Be very careful about going to church, reading your Bible, saying prayers, doing good deeds, and reading books like this through anything but faith in the living Lord. Because the result of all that is belief in a phony Jesus and inoculation to the gospel. You can end up knowing the jargon and playing pretend. Be very careful. Watch your life and your doctrine closely (1 Tim. 4:16). Some of you are so good that you've deceived yourselves. God help you.

On the ground, the gospel comes to us as individuals, as the crowns of God's creation, as people made in his image, and puts before us the prospect of joining the forefront of his restoring of the cosmos. It says something personal about us: "We are rebels." It says something specific about this rebellion: "Christ has made atonement." It holds out a promise requiring individual response: "If you will confess with your mouth that Jesus is Lord and believe in your heart that God raised him from the dead, you will be saved" (Rom. 10:9).

The gospel on the ground, then, reveals the integral narrative we can outline this way: God, man, Christ, response. But this is not the only gospel narrative in the Author's revelation.

PART TWO

The Gospel in the Air

5

Creation

My wife and I like movies. We always have. This has just been one of those things that both she and I like, and I have been lucky that my wife prefers epic movies as opposed to romantic comedies. So when she suggests a movie, it's often something I want to see. I've lucked out in that area of our relationship.

What I really like are the movies that start with one scene and then suddenly move back to the real beginning of the story, explaining how we got to that opening scene. There could be a guy hunkered down, holding his girl; she's bleeding and everybody's crying, and he's firing off rounds at the bad guys, and then all of a sudden he's thinking to himself, "How did I get here?" And then the next scene shows him walking on the beach with a dog, and it kind of throws you off. You're thinking, "What happened?" And then the movie builds back up, showing us all the narrative steps to that opening scene, and we say, "Oh, that's how he got here."

Film and literature critics call the technique used in such opening scenes *in media res*, which is a Latin phrase that basically means "in the middle of the action." Stories that start with events that chronologically occur later in a complete narrative are said to start *in media res*.

In one sense, the gospel on the ground is *in media res*. The immediate gospel of God, man, Christ, response is certainly the thrust of the story, the thick of the action, so to speak. But what the gospel in the air allows us to do is zoom out from the up-close-and-personal viewpoint and still see the narrative of the Scriptures, but this time (to keep with the cinematic analogies) with a wide-angle lens.

Some may argue that to pull back from the gospel on the ground is to lose the real gospel, but what we see in the Bible is a grand story of redemption that, yes, is about us, but is more primarily about God. If we hold to the gospel on the ground only, we commit the cardinal error of dismissing context. The context of the gospel message is not our benefit or our salvation; the context of the gospel is the supremacy of Christ and the glory of God. This story of the good news is personal, but it is also cosmic. In his counsel to gospel preachers, Martyn Lloyd-Jones puts it this way:

> Here, it is important for us to emphasize once more that we must present the total Gospel. There is a personal side to it; we must deal with that, and we must start with that. But we do not stop with that; there is a social side, indeed a cosmic side as well. We must present the whole plan of salvation as it is revealed in the Scriptures. We must show that the ultimate object, as the Apostle Paul puts it in Ephesians 1:10, is to head up in Christ all things, "both which are in heaven, and which are in earth; even in Him."
>
> You are emphasizing that salvation is not merely something subjective, a nice feeling, or peace, or whatever it is they are seeking. All that is important, and is part of it; but there is something more important, namely that the whole universe is involved. We must give the people a conception of this, of the scope and the ambit and the greatness of the gospel in this all-inclusive aspect.[1]

The gospel in the air gives us this conception of the scope and the ambit and the greatness of the gospel. If the Bible gives us a wider context than personal good news for personal sin requiring personal response, let's be faithful to it. At the end of the biblical story, the gospel's star figure says, "Behold, I am making all things new" (Rev. 21:5). If his word is true, we must take his reference to "all things" seriously. As Lloyd-Jones says, "The whole universe is involved."

So let's start out the gospel in the air *in media res*, looking at Romans 8:18–24:

For I consider that the sufferings of this present time are not worth comparing with the glory that is to be revealed to us. For the creation waits with eager longing for the revealing of the sons of God. For the creation was subjected to futility, not willingly, but because of him who subjected it, in hope that the creation itself will be set free from its bondage to corruption and obtain the freedom of the glory of the children of God. For we know that the whole creation has been groaning together in the pains of childbirth until now. And not only the creation, but we ourselves, who have the firstfruits of the Spirit, groan inwardly as we wait eagerly for adoption as sons, the redemption of our bodies.

I love this passage, because it weaves into our concept of creation themes we recognize but don't often think about. We all recognize that things go wrong in the world of nature. We know hurricanes, blizzards, tornados, tsunamis, volcanic eruptions, and the like can be very, very bad. In times of extreme natural disasters, we may wring our hands and wonder whose sin brought it about— not usually ours, but either the gays or the liberals, right?—but we don't often connect basic natural phenomena like flooding and the wildness of animals to fallenness, much less our *own* fallenness. I bet very few people in California, whenever one of their run-of-the-mill earthquakes hits, thinks, "This is because of my sin." But in Romans 8 Paul tells us that creation is eagerly longing, that it's wanting something, that it's desirous of something. He tells us that creation has been subjected to futility, which means that creation has been knocked down from where it *was* to where it is.

In Romans 8 creation groans; it's in the pains of childbirth. Now, I know the pain of childbirth only in a secondary fashion. I've been in the room to see it, but I have not experienced it firsthand. What I can tell you is that I watched my wife go from loving the idea of being able to feel life coming out of her to asking me for an epidural on the way to the hospital. From this experience, I can reasonably deduce that if the pain of childbirth is significant enough that it effectively turns my wife's romantic idea of "Yeah, I love this" into "I don't want to feel this happening," it's got to be pretty heavy. My wife is also very sweet, but at the birth of our first child, she asked me to get out of her face. So in the end, I can safely assume that there is significant pain in childbirth, because I've been in the room with it, and it was scary.

All these sorts of attributes are being lumped into the state of creation, the status of the earth, the mode of the universe. Our world is longing for and in pain about what it's supposed to be. The world isn't sentient, of course; Christians don't believe in some kind of pantheistic notion of the universe's being divine or having a personality. This isn't like *Pocahontas* and the grand-mother tree goddess. But the way Paul develops the metaphor in Romans 8 follows a biblical thread where mountains sing and trees clap (Isa. 55:12), rocks cry (Luke 19:40), and heavens declare (Ps. 19:1). The natural order reacts to the introduction of sin into the world. The world *feels*.

The universe is *in media res*. We've got chaos, we've got bullets, we've got violence, we've got natural disasters, we've got death and disease. And the camera focuses on creation, and creation is think-ing, "Oh man, how did we get here?"

In the Beginning

Our story rushes back to Genesis 1. Let's see how things used to be. The very first verse proclaims, "In the beginning, God created the heavens and the earth." Now let's press Pause.

The Bible is very clear here that in the beginning there was nothing, and the something we have now was created by God. Everything that exists outside of God was brought into existence by God. This is not too obvious a point to illuminate, because there are a lot of people who have big problems with this. They will say that in the face of good science, there's no way that "in the begin-ning, God created everything." Skeptics tell us that science has debunked a literal seven, twenty-four-hour-day creation.

I should put my cards on the table and admit I'm a bit of an agnostic when it comes to science. Scientists change their minds quite often. Their theories evolve more than they say animals do. I'm sure you've noticed the ever-changing studies on what foods or drinks are bad for you. One will say caffeine is bad for the heart, while another will say it's good. Commenting on the ever-evolving discoveries and debunkings in science, after discussing the dueling scientific studies on the alternating benefits and dangers of Vitamin E, chemist Joe Schwarcz writes:

> No one can be certain about what further research will show. But of one thing, I am sure. If I'm around in twenty years to talk about this stuff, I won't be saying the same things as I'm saying now. That's the way science works.[2]

Now, this is not a problem per se for the scientific field. They like discovering new things. Scientists always have a job because there is always new data coming in that helps them refine their research and reconfigure their hypotheses. This is especially true when the accumulating data works against the hypotheses previous data seemed to support.

Kevin Dunbar is a scientist who studied scientists. In the 1990s he commenced an observational study of four different chemistry labs at Stanford University. His results revealed the frustration inherent to scientific pursuit. *Wired* magazine reports:

> Dunbar brought tape recorders into meeting rooms and loitered in the hallway; he read grant proposals and the rough drafts of papers; he peeked at notebooks, attended lab meetings, and videotaped interview after interview. He spent four years analyzing the data. "I'm not sure I appreciated what I was getting myself into," Dunbar says. "I asked for complete access, and I got it. But there was just so much to keep track of."
>
> Dunbar came away from his in vivo studies with an unsettling insight: Science is a deeply frustrating pursuit. Although the researchers were mostly using established techniques, more than 50 percent of their data was unexpected. (In some labs, the figure exceeded 75 percent.) "The scientists had these elaborate theo-

ries about what was supposed to happen," Dunbar says. "But the results kept contradicting their theories. It wasn't uncommon for someone to spend a month on a project and then just discard all their data because the data didn't make sense." Perhaps they hoped to see a specific protein but it wasn't there. Or maybe their DNA sample showed the presence of an aberrant gene. The details always changed, but the story remained the same: The scientists were looking for X, but they found Y.

Dunbar was fascinated by these statistics. The scientific process, after all, is supposed to be an orderly pursuit of the truth, full of elegant hypotheses and control variables. (Twentieth-century science philosopher Thomas Kuhn, for instance, defined normal science as the kind of research in which "everything but the most esoteric detail of the result is known in advance.") However, when experiments were observed up close—and Dunbar interviewed the scientists about even the most trifling details—this idealized version of the lab fell apart, replaced by an endless supply of disappointing surprises. There were models that didn't work and data that couldn't be replicated and simple studies riddled with anomalies. "These weren't sloppy people," Dunbar says. "They were working in some of the finest labs in the world. But experiments rarely tell us what we think they're going to tell us. That's the dirty secret of science."[3]

Other studies pondering the mysterous inefficacy of certain medicines over time lead scientists to begin questioning the very scientific method we teach our elementary-school kids. The scientific method is a system designed to help us make *conclusions*. But the same author of the *Wired* piece, Jonah Lehrer, writes in *The New Yorker* that conclusions can be hard to come by:

> For many scientists, the effect is especially troubling because of what it exposes about the scientific process. If replication is what separates the rigor of science from the squishiness of pseudo-science, where do we put all these rigorously validated findings that can no longer be proved? Which results should we believe? Francis Bacon, the early-modern philosopher and pioneer of the scientific method, once declared that experiments were essential,

because they allowed us to "put nature to the question." But it appears that nature often gives us different answers.[4]

The problem (and the fun) of science is that there's always new data to factor in, often taking the scientist to a new theory, or at least to a new perspective or variation on the old theory. The primary problem is that scientific experiment depends on observation, and until Doc Brown produces the flux capacitor, no scientist can observe the origin of the world. They simply gather the data that's been floating around (for ten thousand to ten billion years, depending on your perspective) after the fact, and hypothesize and hypothesize and hypothesize. And hypothesize some more.

Furthermore, the objectivity of such scientific pursuit is largely a myth. This is not merely a matter of questioning modernistic or naturalistic biases; it is a basic matter of how human beings challenge themselves to think. Karl Popper explains:

> Science . . . cannot start with observations, or with the "collections of data," as some students of method believe. Before we can collect data, our interest in *data of a certain kind* must be aroused: the problem always comes first.[5]

What Popper means is that it is not as if data is just bobbing around in the air like dust mites, and scientists are nonchalantly and unintentionally accumulating it and trying to make sense of it. Scientists have an idea in mind, a problem they wish to solve, or a theory they'd like to develop, and then they begin collecting data with an end in mind. The bottom line is that science is in a constant state of subjectivity and do-overs. When it comes right down to it, science's demand for trust requires at least as much faith as God's demand. Carl Henry concludes:

> The fact is that empirical science has no firm basis whatever on which to raise objections to Christianity, not because scientific and historical concerns are irrelevant to revelation and faith, but because scientists must allow for possible exceptions to every

rule they affirm, and for the empirical vulnerability of the rules themselves.[6]

In other words, science is ever-changing. But our God has no shadow of turning (James 1:17). His everlasting proclamation is firmer than the shifting sands of empirical observation. This is not to say that science is obliterated by Scripture, but rather that it is subsumed by it.

Scientists say that most sufferers of anaplastic oligodendroglioma live only two to three years after diagnosis. They may be right. But they are not factoring in the God of the universe who holds healing in his hands. Science has severe limitations that the God who created all observational data does not. So I think I can be excused when I doubt what scientists are saying today. I'm too afraid of what they'll be saying tomorrow. And I'm foundationally too confident in what God said yesterday.

Godly believers in the gospel who love Jesus equally and want to honor his Word often differ in their views of the origins of the earth. Young-earth creationists and old-earth creationists disagree on the meaning of *day* in the opening verses of Genesis 1, but they agree that what we see was once unseen before God created it (and the eyes to see it) out of nothing. Some Christians believe God spoke the solar system into existence, and some believe God spoke the big bang into existence, which proceeded to form the solar system. In these views and in degrees between them, adherents seek to take the Scriptures seriously and hold to the fact that there once was nothing but God and all that came into being did so by his creative power.

If I had to label myself, I would tend to be more of what's called a "historic creationist." Following from the work of scholars like John Sailhamer—whose book *Genesis Unbound* is brilliant—historic creationists point out that the phrase "in the beginning" in Genesis 1:1 contains the Hebrew word *reshit*, which does not mean a determined piece of time but rather represents the early stages of an unknowable period of time. So in Sailhamer's historic creationism view, "in the beginning God created" refers to a time sometime before the seven days next covered began.

The same Hebrew word "in the beginning" is used to describe Job's early life (Job 8:7). This is clearly not talking about the first day of Job's life but about all of Job's early life, a number of years unshared. That same word *reshit* is also used in Genesis 10:10 to describe King Nimrod's early reign. Once again, a singular day is not in mind here but, rather, an early time *period*. It's seen again in Jeremiah 28:1 to describe the beginning of Zedekiah's reign. So Sailhamer says that the Bible, when it uses this Hebrew term *reshit*, is talking more about an indeterminable amount of time. Historic creationists argue that Genesis doesn't claim that God created the entire universe in those seven days. So when Moses writes in Genesis 1 "In the beginning," he's not saying, "God created all of this in a one-day span."

However, historic creationists absolutely believe that after you get past verses 1 and 2, we are seeing literal twenty-four-hour days, as God grooms a section of land that was uninhabitable ("formless and void") and prepares it for Adam and Eve and places them in the garden and gives them the cultural mandate, "Go and make the rest of the world look like this. You're going to need a lot of help. Have a lot of babies." In my estimation, then, historic creation solves a lot of the tension Christians feel in the Genesis creation account.

Francis Collins, author of *The Language of God* and the chief architect in the Human Genome Project, and his colleagues at the BioLogos Forum argue that we can't read Genesis as a historical narrative but as more of a poetic narrative. It is not historical prose, they say. It is not literal, they say, but *literalistic*. BioLogos believe that evangelicals should embrace the theory of evolution, and they maintain that doing so should offer no challenges to our Christian faith.

The problems with this approach are several, but the primary ones are that it is neither biblical nor very scientific. If we're evolving, the fall makes little sense, because evolution indicates ascendancy, progress. But the fall is just what it says: a fall. On a really basic level, macroevolution violates the second law of thermodynamics, which states that everything is running *down*, not up. The second law of thermodynamics chains creation to entropy and regress, not to evolutionary progress.

Similarly, the concept of evolution violates the first law of thermodynamics, because it is predicated on the introduction of energy into a contained system, and the first law states that this simply doesn't happen. This law of the conservation of energy holds that energy cannot be created or destroyed; it essentially just changes shape. Basically, the first law tells us that nothing in the natural world can come from nothing. So for energy to even exist, the kind of energy necessary for macroevolution to take place, the first law of thermodynamics must be violated *naturally* at several stages throughout the process. The first law points us not to spontaneous development of man from species to species over time, but rather to a creator spontaneously creating *ex nihilo*. Only God could create something from nothing. Douglas Kelly writes:

> The two laws of Thermodynamics indicate the necessity of some power outside present, known processes to have originally brought it all into existence. Something outside and above the vast complex of space, time, energy, material is required to have initiated it; something not relative to it, but free from it (which is the root meaning of the Latin word absolute: "loosed" or "free"—*solutus*, "from"—*ab*). That is, the laws of Thermodynamics can tell us that an absolute creation is necessary.[7]

The assumption of evolution, even with all the power of science's best minds behind it, is tantamount to discovering a watch on a sidewalk and assuming all the elements, pieces, and design came about through natural processes and not from the hands of a watchmaker. Theistic evolutionists have to believe this too, as they argue that God set evolution in motion and the natural processes took over. They have to believe that in order to stay in science's good graces. But evolution doesn't make good sense. Think of something as simple as blood clotting. This process could never have evolved, because prior to the clotting of blood, creatures along the evolutionary chain would have simply died from blood loss. They would not have had a chance to even evolve the ability to survive a wound.

Throughout church history, a variety of perspectives[8]—and often times, no perspectives at all—have arisen on the best exegesis of Genesis 1, but whether you're a historic creationist, young earth creationist, gap-theory advocate, day-age advocate, literary framework advocate, or what-have-you, the clear revelation of Genesis 1 leaves no room for evolutionary descent of mankind. The theory of the evolution of us funky *homo sapiens* doesn't make theological or logical sense. According to many scientists, it doesn't even make scientific sense, although more details in support of that pushback are beyond the scope of this book.[9] The point is that God tells us what he did in the beginning, and if we want to be faithful students of creation, we must begin not with experimental data but with revelation.

Phillip Johnson argues that the New Testament's origin account is more relevant to the evolution controversy than the Old Testament's:

> The place to begin is . . . not in Genesis; rather, it is the opening of the Gospel of John.
>
> > In the beginning was the Word, and the Word was with God, and the Word was God. He was in the beginning with God; all things were made through him, and without him was not anything made that was made. (Jn 1:1–3 RSV)
>
> These simple words make a fundamental statement that is directly contradictory to the corresponding starting point of scientific materialism. Using the Greek word *logos*, the passage declares that in the beginning there was intelligence, wisdom,

and communication. Moreover, this Word is not merely a thing or a concept but a *personal being*.[10]

Why is this important for the evolution controversy? Because, as Johnson notes, "if a personal entity is at the foundation of reality . . . there is more than one way of pursuing knowledge."[11] This puts the Christian interested in honoring God's written Word in an arguably flexible position as it pertains to the age of the earth, but it stands opposed to the theory of the evolutionary development of mankind. How? Because John 1:1–3 tell us there is a personal origin to creation, and when we track that foundation back to the "in the beginning" of Genesis 1, we see that God creates man through the speaking of words into the dust of the ground in the matter of a day, not over billions of years from primordial soup and species to species.

Furthermore, the triune God said that he has made man in his (God's) own image. The transition of man's creation, then, is wholly personal and practically instant. The supremacy of God's proclamation over science's theorization demands this view. The cohesiveness of Christian theology and ministry demands this view. Because we believe in the revelation of God in the written Word and in the incarnation, the resurrection, the indwelling presence of the Holy Spirit, and the miraculous in general, we are supernaturalists *first*, not naturalists. The only reason we feel compelled to accommodate science is that science tells us we ought to. But it is science that should accommodate revelation. Revelation has been around much longer.

We also have to admit up front that the Bible just isn't overly concerned with science. My good friend Mark Driscoll puts it this way:

> In the end, it must be admitted that the age of the earth is simply not stated in the Bible and it may be young or old. Futhermore, both young and old earth advocates are inferring from the Bible a position that the Bible simply does not clearly state. It must

also be admitted that the age of the earth is not a great concern in the Bible; as Augustine rightly said, it is not a scientific text-book seeking to answer the ever-changing inquiries of science, but rather a theological textbook seeking to reveal God and the means by which He saves us.[12]

In the beginning, we start with God's proclamation. God is more interested in declaring than in explaining. In the matter of the creation of the world, the Bible is historical and revelational—it is more interested in telling us what happened and *why* than it is how. God's Word is as clear as God wants it to be about where the world came from (the imagination of God) and why it came to be (to reflect his glory), and its addressing of *how* the world came to be amounts to this: God speaks.

The historic creationism view, however, is biblically and his-torically faithful and leaves room for the proper accommodation of science. "In the beginning," Genesis 1:1 reads. We don't know how long that beginning was. Could it have been billions of years? Maybe. What we do know is that when God began to shape and mold that piece of land for Adam and Eve, the period of prepara-tion lasted seven days.

God created everything that is, and in verses 10, 12, 18, 21, 25, and 31 we find this refrain: ". . . and it was good." Now, don't lose sight of where we started in Romans 8, where there's bullets, blood, death, disease, pain, hurt, longing, and subjection to futility. In the beginning, we've got the earth exulted over with the refrain, ". . . and it was good."

One of the things Lauren and I have tried to impart to our children—one of the things I'm trying to always dial into—is the doctrine of God's creation being good. Very early on, I wanted to tie my daughter's affections to God's goodness in regard to cre-ation. I would tell her, "God thought of the color pink." He didn't have pink in the beginning. He thought that color up. My daughter loves all things pink. So that was one of the conversations we had.

"Where did pink come from?"

"God thought of pink. Isn't that cool?"

When we eat certain foods, I want to be thinking of the fact that the flavor was created by God. In the movie *The Matrix*, they're eating some kind of slop after Neo has been woken up from his false reality. As they're eating this bowl of mush, the characters start asking, "How did the computers know what chicken tastes like? What if they got it wrong? What if chicken was like beef and beef was like chicken?" In the end, what I'm thinking is that God decided, "This tastes like this. And this, when combined with that, forms this flavor. And everything outside of these flavors is going to taste like chicken."

He created the flavors! He created the colors. He created it all, and he did it all out of the overflow of his perfections. It's not like he was thinking, "Oh, I've got some fajita flavoring over here. I know: let's put it on the cow and the chicken." He created the avocado to have a certain flavor; he created the skirt steak, the fillet, and the tenderloin to have certain flavors. That was God's doing. So every aspect of creation, from the largest galaxy to the tiniest burst of flavor in food or drink or seasoning, radiates the goodness of God. Everything declares that "in the beginning, God made me."

The Primacy of God's Glory

As we examine what creation *is*, in all its diversity and wonder, and we ponder how this creation came to be, we must remember that all the complexity and beauty in the universe is not meant to terminate on itself but to trace its origin to the Creator. We have examined the *what* of creation and touched a little bit on the *how*, but the *why* still remains.

God created everything, and what he created was good, but what he created to be good was not created as an end in itself but was given to us as good in order that we might be driven to worship him. In other words, when you and I take a bite of food, that should spark worship in us—not a worship of food, of course, but of the Creator of food. When you and I feel the warmth of our child hugging us, that should create worship in us. When we feel the warmth of the sun on our faces, that should create worship. When we smell the rain, that should create worship. We could go on and on. The goodness of creation is designed not to declare itself but to act as a signpost pointing heavenward. This is why Paul can say, "So, whether you eat or drink, or whatever you do, do all to the glory of God" (1 Cor. 10:31). He is working from the assumption that anything we do can be done to the glory of God.

We are never *not* worshiping, anyway. It is easy to see that you and I have been created to worship. We're flat-out desperate for it. From sports fanaticism to celebrity tabloids to all the other strange sorts of voyeurisms now normative in our culture, we evidence that we were created to look at something beyond ourselves and marvel at it, desire it, like it with zeal, and love it with affection. Our thoughts, our desires, and our behaviors are always oriented around something, which means we are always worshiping— ascribing worth to—something. If it's not God, we are engaging in idolatry. But either way, there is no way to turn the worship switch in our hearts off. Tim Keller writes:

> When your meaning in life is to fix someone else's life, we may call it "co-dependency" but it is really idolatry. An idol is what- ever you look at and say, in your heart of hearts, "If I have that, then I'll feel my life has meaning, then I'll know I have value, then I'll feel significant and secure." There are many ways to describe that kind of relationship to something, but perhaps the best one is *worship*.[13]

In fact, any time we orient our heart of hearts around some- thing, we are worshiping that thing. The aim of the Scriptures is to direct our worship to the one true God of the universe, and the universe itself is designed not to occupy our worship but to stir our heart of hearts to behold its God. The heavens do not declare the glory of themselves, after all, but the glory of God.

So creation draws us to look at something beyond ourselves and marvel at it. All of creation has been given to us so that we behold the awesome God who has made it all and made it all good. John Calvin writes:

> Ever since in the creation of the universe he brought forth those insignia whereby he shows his glory to us, whenever and wherever we cast our gaze. . . . And since the glory of his power and wisdom shine more brightly above, heaven is often called his palace. Yet . . . wherever you cast your eyes, there is no spot in the universe wherein you cannot discern at least some sparks of his glory.[14]

The responsibility this puts on us is to exercise dominion over creation for the glory of God, not for the glory of ourselves or for creation itself. Because God declared his creation good, we have a responsibility to steward creation well, not as servants to it but as servants to God. This makes what we often call "creation care" a valid aspect of being responsible stewards of God's good gift, but it makes creation worship way outside the bounds of acceptability. So those who place the natural world, be it flora or fauna, at a higher value than human beings are engaging in idolatry. Likewise, anyone who places the object of worship—whether they call it "god" or "goddess" or anything else—within creation itself, is engaging in idolatry. From this sort of worship dysfunction we get everything from New Age spirituality to pantheism to anarchic eco-terrorism. Anybody who wants to burn down a building to save trees or harpoon a sailor to save whales is captive to a perverted worship.

But we were meant to worship, meant to give glory to something greater than ourselves. So we interact with the earth in such a way that our hearts and minds should always be being stirred up to how good, beautiful, and gracious God is to us in what he's given, from his creativity in crafting flavors, to his beneficence in dispensing the warmth of the sun. The scriptural testimony is consistently this: God's chief concern is for his own glory. As we learned in chapter 1, the main point of the Bible is God's glorious self-regard. Therefore, the main point of human life ought to be regard of God's glory.

I'm guessing most of you reading this book will eat at least three meals today, or at least be able to if you so desire. What is often lost on almost every one of us is that most of the rest of the world doesn't get to do that. So instead of a trite little "Thank you, God" prayer to bless our food, why don't we really dial in and say, "Thank you, God, that you provide this, that you provide in a way that requires very little effort or strain on my part, and that you could take it away any second but haven't"? How about a gratitude for the provision of God on top of a gratitude for the creative glory of God in flavors and how it all comes together?

That is the point of God's creation. That is the point of creation's goodness. Our recognition of, and reveling in, the glory of God.

How the Present Shadows the Past

We can still see in the Scriptures after the fall that God's plan for redemption encompasses more than just individual reconciliation to God. What we get when we lop off the context of the gospel in the air from the whole scriptural narrative is that sort of sentimental cliché that says the Bible is God's love letter to you. In one way, this is true, but Rick Warren was on to something when he opened his best-selling book with "It's not about you"[15] and subtitled it *What on Earth Am I Here For?*. We see throughout the Scriptures that the fuller gospel story has in view something larger than just our fulfillment, our security, our joy, and our personal relationship with God.

One of the unintentional errors of staying in the gospel on the ground too long is an over-individualizing of the gospel, but what we see from the air is that God's creative goodness, which is fractured by the fall but which the gospel in the air reveals as his plan to restore, is greater than an individual believer. We see glimpses of this wider order in Scripture signposts even after the fall. In the present brokenness, we can see shadows of the past peace.

We may see this first in the account of the first murder, in Genesis 4. Adam and Eve's son Cain killed his younger brother Abel out of jealousy over God's acceptance of Abel's sacrifice. When God comes for a reckoning, he asks Cain, "Where is Abel?" to which Cain replies, "Am I my brother's keeper?" (v. 9). In Cain's reply is an implicit pledge of self-allegiance. "I'm my own person," Cain is saying. "I'm not responsible for anybody else." But also implicit in the reply is the fruit of fallenness, because God's design is for us to be responsible for each other, to live not for ourselves but for God and others. Cain's self-centered response reveals the radical individualism inherent in the fall but also the radical other-centeredness that existed before the fall and that will be restored by the gospel in the new heavens and the new earth.

We see this design in the Ten Commandments, for instance. The first four commandments correspond to our vertical relationship with God. The remaining commandments correspond to our horizontal relationship with our neighbors. The law reflects in shadow what the gospel brings in light: reconciliation between sinners and God, and between sinners and each other. Jesus makes this direct in the Great Commandment when he combines "Love the Lord your God with all your heart, soul, mind, and strength" with "Love your neighbor as yourself" (Matt. 22:37–39). The command addresses what the gospel will restore. We even see this wider scope of reconciliation in Paul's words about the reconciling gospel bestowing upon believers the ministry of reconciliation (2 Cor. 5:11–21); the gospel does not terminate on individual salvation. Its aim is bigger, broader. It aims to restore "all things," including brotherhood.

Back in the Old Testament laws, we find stipulations about how to feed animals and let them rest and how to let the land *itself* rest after it's been harvested so many times. There are commonsense reasons for these requirements, of course, but hidden beneath them is a pointing to both the brokenness in the natural order and a time of unbrokenness in history past. Even the decline in life spans we see throughout the Old Testament points us to a time when life was epic. It reminds us that our bodies were good.

The miracles of Jesus are signs of the right order of things. Jesus was not so much turning things upside down as turning them rightside up or, at least, giving his followers glimpses of the rightside up. The miracles of healing, deliverance, provision, and resurrection all reveal that God, through Jesus, is making all things new, that he is restoring what once was unbroken. The very phrase "gospel of the kingdom," which is the summation of what Jesus and his disciples preached, points us to something larger than just individual salvation. And while individual salvation is at the tipping point of God's gospel—the kingdom is in the midst of us, after all (Luke 17:21)—the designation *kingdom* itself tells us that the gospel is God's plan not just to restore mankind, but to restore "all things" for mankind's enjoyment, Christ's lordship, and his triune self's glory.

Haywire

Several years ago, I was preaching out of Ephesians 2 in front of about twelve hundred people on the doctrine of total depravity, which is the idea that we are born sinful. Sin isn't something that happens to us when we figure out right and wrong. Intrinsic within our being is rebellion. All you have to do to believe this is watch children. Children don't have to be taught violence. Children will bite one another to get what they want. They don't learn that from their environment; it's inside of them. Children are horrifically selfish; they don't have to be taught that. Selfishness is not an environmentally learned behavior. So I was teaching this: "Hey, we are brought forth in iniquity. We are born rebellious. We are born, in essence, evil."

In the middle of my talk, a young woman started waving at me, trying to get my attention. My primary play in such circumstances is to just ignore it and let security handle it, so I just kept preaching. But she started waving both arms at me, so I finally stopped and said, "Yes ma'am?" She stood up and couldn't have been more than fifteen years old. She said, "Do you have any children?"

I said, "I don't. I don't have any children."

She said, "Then don't tell me my baby's evil."

Talk about an awkward moment. I just asked some questions. "Tell me about your baby. Is it a boy or a girl? How old is he?" I found out the backstory later, that she was fourteen years old when she got pregnant and gave birth, and she was living with her grandparents because her folks had kicked her out of the house. It was just a messy situation. So I decided to talk to her about her son.

"Tell me about him. Does he always listen to you? Has he bitten a kid yet? Does he ever hit anybody?" That kind of thing.

Her answers indicated that, yes, of course, contrary to her own nice behavior and correction, her son consistently chose to inflict harm on others and disobey her rules.

I lovingly walked her through this reality and said, "You see? That's a rebellious spirit that's intrinsic within him."

She seemed fine and sat down, and I thought everything was cool. I went back to preaching. But about five minutes later, a grown woman in the back starts waving her hands up in the air. I couldn't believe it. I said, "Yes ma'am?"

She said, "I agree with her."

So I said, "Okay, let's just do this. If anyone can give me any verse in the Bible that supports the default innocence of human beings, let's talk about it. But there is a way that seems right to you that in the end leads to death (Prov. 14:12; 16:25). So if you want to talk about what the Bible teaches, we can have that conversation all day. But if you're saying, 'I don't care what the Bible teaches,' then we can't really have this conversation, because you and I see the world through completely different lenses. You're arguing upon what you think, and I'm arguing on thousands upon thousands of years of theology and God's self-revealed will. But if you want to talk Scripture, let's talk Scripture."

I figured I was making a deal with the crowd. And in my mind, I started to line up as many verses on the doctrine of total depravity in my head as I could think of. I started to prepare my defenses. The lady thought she had me nailed right out of the gate. She responded to my challenge: "That's easy. Genesis 1 says God made it and it was good."

It was like she'd set the ball on a tee in front of me. With as much love and tenderness as I had in my heart, I said, "You're absolutely right. God made the world and he declared it all good. But there's this thing that happens in Genesis 3 that changes all of that."

This is how we get to the *in media res* of Romans 8. Genesis 3 is where everything goes haywire. And when I say everything, I mean *everything*. Sin enters the world and fractures all the beauty, all the goodness, and all the peace previously established at every level of creation and society. I'd love to live in Genesis 1 and 2. There's no subjection to futility there, no bondage to corruption, no slavery to death. There's none of that. That would be a dream; that would be beautiful. But it's not the world you and I live in. It's not where our children grow up, it's not where we work, and it's not where we live. God created the world and made it good. But thereafter something terrible happened.

6

Fall

Sin is cosmic treason.

R. C. SPROUL[1]

The world was made for God's glory, but his glory in creation was made manifest in man and woman, bearers of his image, who were created to take dominion over creation, to be the crown jewel of the material world. So when sin entered us, it entered the world. Original sin has effects beyond humanity; it affects the world, the cosmos. "The whole creation has been groaning" (Rom. 8:22). This is not just to remind us of the seriousness of rebellion against God but to indicate that human rebellion against God disrupts the natural order of everything. This is why a whole gospel must be explicitly about the restoration of God's image bearers and also about the restoration of the entire theater of his glory, the entire cosmos.

We see this important connection between Adam's disobedience and the fall of the very earth itself in Genesis 3, as God pronounces the curse:

And to Adam he said,
"Because you have listened to the voice of your wife
    and have eaten of the tree
of which I commanded you,
    'You shall not eat of it,'
cursed is the ground because of you;
    in pain you shall eat of it all the days of your life;

thorns and thistles it shall bring forth for you;
    and you shall eat the plants of the field.
By the sweat of your face
    you shall eat bread,
till you return to the ground,
    for out of it you were taken;
for you are dust,
    and to dust you shall return." (vv. 17–19)

The harmony that Adam and Eve enjoyed with God's creation, the peaceful dominion they were given over it, is now broken. "Cursed is the ground because of you." The fracture between Adam and creation reflects the fracture between God and Adam. Where Adam's work was toil-less, it is now toilsome. While the earth was once wonderfully subdued, it now yields grudgingly. Where it was once only fruitful and abundant, it now offers the challenge of thorns and thistles. And while Adam was once bestowed with imperishable flesh, his sin limits the life span of his body. Having rejected God's blessings, he has chosen to place his hope in the dust from which he was fashioned.

Adam and Eve were placed as the crowns of God's good creation, but as the crown goes, so goes the creation. Their sin brings the curse to us all, and the curse is found far as east is from west. What Adam and Eve enjoyed before the fall is often referred to by the Hebrew word *shalom*. Scholar Cornelius Plantinga explains:

The webbing together of God, humans, and all creation in justice, fulfillment, and delight is what the Hebrew prophets call *shalom*. We call it peace, but it means far more than mere peace of mind or a cease-fire between enemies. In the Bible, shalom means *universal flourishing, wholeness, and delight*—a rich state of affairs in which natural seeds are satisfied and natural gifts fruitfully employed, a state of affairs that inspires joyful wonder as its Creator and Savior opens doors and welcomes the creatures in whom he delights. Shalom, in other words, is the way things ought to be.[2]

The order God established in creating the universe and us as its inhabitants is certainly reflected in the law—it is there summarized in the command to the first humans not to eat of the tree of the knowledge of good and evil—but it is bigger than legal commands. It is a system of order, the state of all things. *Shalom* is the word for when the state of things is in harmony with God's holiness. When there was *shalom*, Adam and Eve stewarded the creation God had given them in a way that accurately reflected God's glory. The way they cultivated the garden, tirelessly drawing forth from it the best fruit, was a reflection of the way God at no exertion to himself drew forth Adam and Eve's best. The whole place ran like a machine well oiled with the joy of the Lord.

Their sin, however, threw a wrench in the gears. We see how the relationship between humanity and the garden is broken when the relationship between humanity and God is broken:

> Therefore the LORD God sent him out from the garden of Eden to work the ground from which he was taken. He drove out the man, and at the east of the garden of Eden he placed the cherubim and a flaming sword that turned every way to guard the way to the tree of life. (Gen. 3:23–24)

The way back in is blocked. *Shalom* has been shattered. The aftereffects are cataclysmic and far-reaching. Tim Keller writes:

> Human beings are so integral to the fabric of things that when human beings turned from God the entire warp and woof of the world unraveled. . . . We have lost God's shalom—physically, spiritually, socially, psychologically, culturally. Things now fall apart.[3]

Perhaps we see this unraveled fabric most explored and most lamented in the Old Testament book of Ecclesiastes.

Ecclesiastes and the Blocked Garden

In his classic novel *Moby Dick*, Herman Melville wrote that "Ecclesiastes is the fine hammered steel of woe," and that this work attributed to Solomon is "the truest of all books."[4] He is saying that we can trust Ecclesiastes because of the sorrow in it. We can trust a man who's lived hard. He has nothing to lose, so it can be expected he'd shoot us straight.

This is not the inclination of our world, which makes an idol of success. We are desperate for success. There are companies whose sole job is to motivate you to be successful. Have you ever seen the "Successories" products? They include those now-iconic posters that say things like "Teamwork" with a little phrase underneath. (I like even more the posters that mock the Successories posters; they are called Demotivators.[5] One of my favorites features a photo of a ship sinking, and the caption reads, "Sometimes the journey of a thousand miles ends very, very, very badly.")

People eat this stuff up. I've never met the guy who said, "I don't want to be successful." Whether it's in business or in life or in family or in relationships, we all want to have some measure of success. Churches today recognize this and orient their entire mission around people's felt need for success. The message is that to be outside the success circle is somehow not to be normal or blessed, that real victory is synonymous with some kind of earthly, practical, material success.

The Bible does address success, of course. More specifically, the Bible addresses notions of success in these five books that stand together in the middle of the Old Testament. They're called the "Wisdom Literature": Job, Psalms, Proverbs, Ecclesiastes, and Song of Solomon. Each one of the books carries its own purpose.

The book of Proverbs is a kind of field guide to success; it addresses everything from money to relationships to character. The Psalms, one of my personal favorites, features some of the writings of the great schizophrenic king, David. (I think he's schizophrenic, because in one line he will say, "How long, Oh Lord, will you forsake me?" and then two lines later he will say something like, "How great you are to be so near to me." But my soul resonates with that.) The psalms contain quite a few songs of victory. The Song of Solomon is a book about the celebration of marital sex. That's some sweet success!

Now we've got two books left in the Wisdom Literature—Job and Ecclesiastes. These two books form one lesson from two opposite ends of the spectrum. Job demonstrates the depths of human suffering and proclaims the depths of God's glory in a very personal way. The book of Job brings the microscope to brokenness and deliverance the way Genesis 2 brings the microscope to creation. Ecclesiastes, like Genesis 1, gives us a telescope view.

People who have Job-like experiences may moan, "Well, if life wasn't like this, if I had more money, if I had more power, if I had more friends, if I had better religion . . ." or, "If my parents weren't so mean, if I had grown up in a different place . . ." What they begin to create in their minds is the idea that a better existence exists somewhere over the rainbow. The problem with that is Ecclesiastes.

Ecclesiastes 1:1 tells us that this book contains "the words of the Preacher." The identifier is sometimes translated "Teacher." Right out of the gate we learn that this book is more than just a life story; it is the chronicle of a lesson learned. "The words of the Preacher [or Teacher], the son of David, king in Jerusalem." The author is Solomon. This man is the king of a prosperous, wealthy, powerful nation. He has more wealth, power, and fame than you will ever, ever, ever have. He is more educated. This isn't just some guy off the street. He is beyond us in terms of education, wealth, and power. And in verse 2, he writes, "Vanity of vanities, says the Preacher, vanity of vanities!"

Now, this word *vanity* in the Hebrew has the sense of "meaningless." What a chipper introduction to his book, eh? "Meaningless, meaningless, meaningless." We can all look at life and agree that there are some parts that have no purpose—like neckties or cats. But Solomon is going to take it a step further, and he's going to tell us that *everything* in life is meaningless. "Vanity of vanities, says the Preacher, vanity of vanities! All is vanity." He is not just saying, "This particular thing bothers me." He says, "Everything is meaningless."

"Everything, Solomon?"

"Everything."

"What about marriage?"

"Meaningless."

"What about pleasure?"

"Meaningless."

"What about wealth?"

"Meaningless. Everything under the sun—everything that is— is meaningless."

I read this and chuckle and want to hug him. I want to hug him and have him in my house and assure him, "It will be all right, Solomon." But he is going to methodically, over the course of twelve chapters, talk about every aspect of living and then attach worthlessness to it.

In fact, through all twelve chapters of Ecclesiastes, he will use the Hebrew word *hebel* ("meaningless") thirty-eight times. Why does he come at the problem in such a cynical way? Why is his pessimism so pervasive? In Ecclesiastes 1:3 he writes, "What does man gain by all the toil at which he toils under the sun?" This is why Solomon says the sum of all of life's accumulated experiences is meaninglessness: for all of our work, we die and leave this place unchanged. For all that we accomplish, whether you get up at 5:00 and hit the ground running or you sleep in till 10:00, no matter what you do, you die and leave this place unchanged. Look at what Solomon writes in 1:4–7:

A generation goes, and a generation comes,
    but the earth remains forever.
The sun rises, and the sun goes down,
    and hastens to the place where it rises.
The wind blows to the south
    and goes around to the north;

around and around goes the wind,
    and on its circuits the wind returns.
All streams run to the sea,
    but the sea is not full;
to the place where the streams flow,
    there they flow again.

He's describing life as if it's a treadmill! We get caught up in this silly circular pattern, and at the end of the day, each generation runs with all the vigor of the sweaty man on the treadmill at the gym. And when all is said and done, we don't go anywhere.

Let me give you some little examples. No matter how hard you work, there's always laundry, isn't there? No matter how many times you wash it, it's dirty again. I had to mow the lawn yesterday. I just did it a week ago. And next week I'll have to do it again. I had to get my hair cut this week, even though I got my hair cut a month ago. It grew back. I have to pay the same bills every month. Are we sensing a theme here? Solomon is trying to tell us, "It's all exhausting because it doesn't matter." He writes in verse 8, "All things are full of weariness; a man cannot utter it; the eye is not satisfied with seeing, nor the ear filled with hearing."

Tomorrow morning, the alarm will go off at 6:30. You will wake up, shower, get dressed, and get in your car. You will stop at Starbucks, sit in traffic, get to your office or cubicle or workstation (which just means you're in a closet). At lunch, you will eat something, probably with some friends. After lunch, you will go back to your workstation/cubicle/office/shop/classroom/whatever, and you will work until 5:00 or 6:00. You will then leave work, maybe go to the gym, but probably not. You will go home, you will eat dinner, you will watch a little television, and you will go to bed. And then you'll do the very same thing the next day. Life is more like the film *Groundhog Day* than anyone wants to admit. We're trapped. We're blocked out of the garden. We're in a rut, just toiling under the sun.

Some people, though, like to pretend this isn't the case. Let me show you how they do it, by taking a look at Ecclesiastes 1:9–10:

> What has been is what will be,
>> and what has been done is what will be done,
>> and there is nothing new under the sun.
>
> Is there a thing of which it is said,
>> "See, this is new"?
>
> It has been already
>> in the ages before us.

Solomon is basically saying there's no such thing as *new*. You think you've found a way out, a way that's different from the rut, but you haven't. It's been tried already and found wanting. The shiny distractions of new things are a deceptive part of the circular silliness. We see this play out in life over and over and over again. The new gadget or a new wardrobe or a new house or a new boat or a new car promises a weird relief and excitement, doesn't it? Have you ever thought about how weird that is? A new cell phone, the cool one, makes you feel better. This kind of consumerism comes with an emotional stroking, like a narcotic high. But then it wears off. New stuff becomes old stuff really quickly, and we need the next new thing. The Scriptures are saying, "Give me a break. Trinkets are trinkets."

Let's not deceive ourselves. Nothing we think of as new is going to give us a way out of the brokenness. That stuff is all meaningless. No change of job, no increased income, no new home, no new electronic device, or no new spouse is going to make things better inside of you. This is what Solomon is lamenting.

This sobering outlook has huge implications for the ambitious among us. The alpha males out there are thinking, "Not me. I will change the known universe. I will do such a great job in business and such a phenomenal job with my family that the memory of me will live on for generations." Check out Ecclesiastes 1:11: "There is no remembrance of former things, nor will there be any remembrance of later things yet to be among those who come after." Solomon's answer amounts to, "Umm, no. You're going to die, and no one's going to remember you." Do you know your great-great-great-great-great-great grandfather's name? It wasn't *that* long ago. Do you know your great-great-great grandfather's name? See what I mean?

In Ecclesiastes 1:12–13 we read, "I the Preacher have been king over Israel in Jerusalem. And I applied my heart to seek and to search out by wisdom all that is done under heaven." You'll remember that when David died and Solomon became king, God offered Solomon anything he wanted. What did Solomon want? Wisdom. He didn't ask for wealth, he didn't ask for power—he said, "I want wisdom. I want to be the smartest man alive." God thought it was an honorable request. Afterward, Solomon set out to discover "all that is done under heaven." He used his five senses, along with all his wealth, power, and wisdom, to engage absolutely everything the world has to offer. And when all was said and done, he said it's absolutely meaningless.

"I said in my heart, 'I have acquired great wisdom, surpassing all who were over Jerusalem before me, and my heart has had great experience of wisdom and knowledge'" (v. 16).

Basically he's saying, "In case you think I'm a liar, let me remind you of this. I'm smarter than you, more powerful than you, and have more women than you." Solomon has been there, done that, and burnt the T-shirt. We should trust him on this stuff; he knows what he's talking about. "And I applied my heart to know wisdom and to know madness and folly. I perceived that this also is but a striving after wind" (v. 17). He has tried everything, and everything has come up lacking. It was about as satisfying as chasing the wind.

Solomon has left no stone unturned in his search for satisfaction, and no experience or wisdom the world has to offer has scratched the itch. He has far exceeded the pinnacles of success in every area, and yet he never gets there. He can never be there, because once he's there, it becomes *here* and another there awaits. The cycle is endless. The pursuit is meaningless.

Until we honestly evaluate this life under the sun, until we are ready to look at our lives and see that the real meaning lies outside the world's system, we will be stuck on the treadmill. This place is broken. There's no sense in looking into it for the fix.

We are exiled from the garden into a wasteland, and we keep thinking we can make this wasteland into the garden. But that doesn't work and never will. What has been lost is too great for us to recover on our own; the chasm is too wide for our feeble efforts to bridge.

Ecclesiastes and the Loss of *Shalom*

We have a *shalom*-shaped hole in our hearts, and no matter how much we throw in there, and no matter how long we try filling it, nothing will satisfy but *shalom* itself. Everybody knows something's broken in the world. But illogically, foolishly, we are looking for fixes from broken people with broken ideas in broken places.

My favorite definition of sin comes from a philosopher named Søren Kierkegaard, who, in *The Sickness unto Death*, writes, "Sin is: in despair not wanting to be oneself before God."[6] In essence, Kierkegaard is saying that sin is building your self-worth on anything other than God. This is the DNA of sin. This view certainly makes the root of sin more pervasive and the temptation to sin more dangerous. We can place our self-worth in anything, including otherwise good things. When we take a good thing and make it an ultimate thing, we ensure that that thing will drive us into the ground.

I'll give you one example. You can make money the ultimate goal of your life. There's nothing inherently wrong with money or possessions; otherwise God wouldn't tell us not to steal each other's stuff. But you can spend all your time on money, putting all your energy into accumulating it. You can buy a house that you rarely get to go into because you're working fifteen-hour days so you can amass a fortune. But in the end, you're going to be painted up like a clown, put in a box, and buried. I'm not being crass; I'm just being honest. Vanity, vanity—it's all vanity.

Or how about something more spiritual? Take religion, for another instance. Religion practiced apart from faith in Christ is called *self-righteousness* in the Bible, and not even the perfecters of self-righteousness themselves, the Pharisees, qualified for God's kingdom. Faithless religion is vanity. No matter how many people it practically helps, no matter how good it makes you feel, religious effort not rooted in the gospel is rooted in self-justifying self-worth. This is meaningless.

What are we looking for in all these idolatrous efforts at self-worth? *Shalom.* We want to experience that God-ordained harmony once again, even if we don't know we do. J. R. R. Tolkien says we are wired to yearn for the garden: "Certainly there was an Eden on this very unhappy earth. We all long for it, and we are constantly glimpsing it: our whole nature at its best and least corrupted, its gentlest and most humane, is still soaked with the sense of 'exile.'"[7]

Arguably, no book of the Bible illustrates both the frustration and the longing of this sense of exile like Solomon's Ecclesiastes. What do we first think to do when we feel our loss of peace? We seek pleasure. Solomon did the same:

> I said in my heart, "Come now, I will test you with pleasure; enjoy yourself." But behold, this also was vanity. I said of laughter, "It is mad," and of pleasure, "What use is it?" I searched with my heart how to cheer my body with wine—my heart still guiding me with wisdom—and how to lay hold on folly, till I might see what was good for the children of man to do under heaven during the few days of their life. (Eccles. 2:1–3)

He's saying, "I'm going to devote myself to pleasure," and he begins to systematically throw the largest parties the world has ever seen. He is going to have comedians brought in: he's inviting Dave Chappelle, Dane Cook, and those redneck guys that are so popular right now (for reasons that I don't quite understand). He brings in the funny men at the top of their games, hosts them with the best food, barrels of the best wine, and palaces decorated by the best party planners. Solomon is getting after it, seven days a week for an extended period of time. His parties were epic.

You may be thinking, "He partied, sure. But did he par-tay?" Look at 1 Kings 4:22–23: "Solomon's provision for one day was thirty cors of fine flour [that's 220 liters, for those of you who like the metric system] and sixty cors of meal, ten fat oxen, and twenty pasture-fed cattle, a hundred sheep, besides deer, gazelles, roe-bucks, and fattened fowl." Every commentary I read converts this to the same numbers: Solomon was putting on parties for between fifteen- and twenty-thousand people. So that little barbecue soirée, that little kegger you had in your backyard, is preschool.

Eventually, though, he got tired of waking up in the back of a chariot on his way to Mexico with a new tattoo, so he moved on from there to think, "I've got to make something of my life. Man, all I'm doing is partying, all I'm doing is eating great food and drinking wine and being everybody's buddy. I can't keep sleeping to 11:00. I need to make something of myself."

Look at what he does next: "I made great works. I built houses and planted vineyards for myself. I made myself gardens and parks, and planted in them all kinds of fruit trees. I made myself pools from which to water the forest of growing trees" (Eccles. 2:4–6). He has decided to cut back on the partying and to try being a bit more constructive.

To give you an idea of the kind of activity we're talking about here, the temple that Solomon built took seven years to construct. It was ornate, covered with gold and precious stones, and considered one of the wonders of the ancient world. Solomon's house, in comparison, took fourteen years to build. Not only that, but he builds houses for all his wives, which is a feat in itself.

What is his purpose with all this? A sense of both pride and permanence occurs when you finally own a home. When you leave the apartment and you finally get that house, there's this feeling of permanence, of having *arrived*. There is also something that happens to the soul of someone who works outside all day to build something. Our souls are hardwired to resonate with this kind of work, because it resembles God's original mandate to Adam to subdue the earth, to take dominion over it. When you landscape your yard, plant a garden, and get your hands dirty in the dirt and grass so that everything looks great, and you step back and look at it, saying, "Oh man, this looks beautiful," you're tapping into that preexilic feeling.

But Solomon, not to be outdone, says, "Yeah, I didn't plant a garden; I planted a *forest*. I like what you've done with the pansies and the geraniums, but I planted a forest." He goes well beyond what most of us can even comprehend. Solomon isn't some Home Depot weekend warrior. In fact, to this day, if you go to southwest Jerusalem, you will come to a place where there are all these craters in the earth, and it's called the Pools of Solomon. This is where Solomon dug cavernous holes in the earth and filled them with water to irrigate all the national parks and everything else he built. But he says even this massive beautification was meaningless. (And we think putting in a koi pond or a water feature will help us find tranquility.) What's next?

> I bought male and female slaves, and had slaves who were born in my house. I had also great possessions of herds and flocks, more than any who had been before me in Jerusalem. I also gathered for myself silver and gold and the treasure of kings and provinces. I got singers, both men and women, and many concubines, the delight of the children of man. (Eccles. 2:7–8)

Solomon basically became Billy Madison. He's saying, "I didn't do anything for myself. I woke up about 11:00, and somebody cooked breakfast for me, chewed it up for me, and then fed it to me. I moved on from there to get a massage. I moved on from there to get the facial, the pedicure . . ." He tried partying and building, and now he's trying just taking it easy. He tried the Richie Rich scene. He tried the polo club scene. He tried the music scene. If he liked a certain song, he didn't download the MP3; he bought the band. On top of all this, he indulged in what he's infamous for: women. Solomon had seven hundred wives. Now, there isn't any way to keep seven women happy, much less seven hundred. But he had seven hundred wives and three hundred concubines at his beck and call. This is not big love; it's big lust. Solomon experienced uninhibited sexuality. He made Hugh Hefner look like an amateur.

Solomon tries everything, and he tries it bigger and better than anybody ever has. This did not escape notice. Check out Ecclesiastes 2:9: "So I became great and surpassed all who were before me in Jerusalem." Do you hear what he's saying? "I was popular." Is it any wonder? After such huge parties, such massive landscaping projects, such vast wealth, and such sexual prowess, is it any wonder he became the most famous man of his day? All five hundred million people on Facebook would have "liked" him. He'd be on the cover of every magazine. He was like Einstein, JFK, and Justin Bieber all rolled into one.

But what he says in the second part of Ecclesiastes 2:9 is really intriguing: "Also my wisdom remained with me." What does he mean? I believe he means that he never forgot what he was doing. He never got so caught up in seeking pleasure that he forgot that his goal was, from the beginning, to see if there was really anything of value out there in the world. From day one, he never forgot that this was an experiment. It may be easy to say, "Well, if you indulge in such a way that you're out of control, of course you won't find satisfaction." But Solomon indulged in all of this stuff very heavily, all the while maintaining his wisdom. He never lost sight that he was intentionally seeking meaning in his indulgences. So he had the best of both worlds going on here. He could act like an addict but keep his wits about him somehow.

You and I cannot do this, mainly because we don't have the

unparalleled wisdom that God gave Solomon. In any event, the bottom line is not that Solomon sought pleasure but didn't find it. He *did* find it. He says, "And whatever my eyes desired I did not keep from them. I kept my heart from no pleasure, for my heart found pleasure in all my toil" (Eccles. 2:10).

Solomon is saying, "The party scene . . . I'm not going to lie to you. I had a good time, man." The building of the houses and the pools, the planting of the gardens, the great food and wine, the lavish parties, the best bands, an abundance of women, the money and the stuff—Solomon had a great time. Then verse 11: "Then I considered all that my hands had done and the toil I had expended in doing it, and behold, all was vanity and a striving after wind, and there was nothing to be gained under the sun."

Don't miss this point! The *shalom*-shaped hole in our hearts cannot be filled with anything but God's *shalom*.

Solomon ran out of fantasies. Anything he could think up in his head, he did. He played it all out. In the end, he had done everything there is to do, and he found himself back in the same place he had been before he ever started this pursuit, feeling that life is boring and predictable and being a little frustrated and on edge because of it.

The powerful irony of this frustration is that God is the author of every good thing. Pleasure, partying, gardens, work, money, material things, and sex are all his ideas. Adam and Eve were created and set in the garden wearing nothing. That's a great deal! I love the way God started the whole thing: one man, one woman, a bunch of acreage, and naked. "Go, play, frolic, and have a good time." This is what *shalom* looked like! Somehow we have received the idea that God is a cosmic killjoy, but we stand on Scripture to say that this deep longing in the core of who we are that cries out for happiness and delight was put there by him and *he means for us to be satisfied.*

We pursue this satisfaction from day one. In this fallen world, we come out of the womb desperate for *shalom*. From the second we are born, we seek our own happiness, don't we? At 4:00 a.m., in the middle of the night, the middle of the afternoon, in a church service, or during Grandma's funeral, it doesn't matter: "Give me a bottle. Give me my thumb. Give me some food. Entertain me. Dance for me. Make those funny faces." We pop out snapping our fingers for satisfaction, and we never really stop.

This need never changes, even as the pursuit does. It may look different the older we get, but the desire is always the same. We seek our own happiness, our own pleasure. It is the motivating factor behind everything we do, always. But it is not the need that is wrong; it is the array of ways apart from Jesus that we search out to meet it. Solomon's words, then, are a vivid reminder of how deep, deep, deep our void goes. They illustrate for us just how far-gone *shalom* is. But Solomon has done us a great service. Ecclesiastes is in the Bible so that nothing would be in our heart but Jesus.

The Search as Sense

Every person is searching for meaning, significance, and happiness. Whatever label we put on it, however we identify it, we all are looking for fulfillment. And this search for fulfillment alone should tell us that there is an actual fulfillment to be had.

In the 1600s, there was a freak-show genius-mathematician-philosopher-theologian named Blaise Pascal, who said:

> All men seek happiness. This is without exception. Whatever different means they employ, they all tend to this end. The cause of some going to war, and of others avoiding it, is the same desire in both, attended with different views. The will never takes the least step but to this object. This is the motive of every action of every man, even of those who hang themselves.[8]

Happiness is the driving force behind everything you do. Anything you do has the desire for happiness at its center. Even distasteful things we do are done because we see them ultimately as preferable and more conducive to happiness than the alternatives. As a parent, I can tell you one of the worst things is taking our kids for shots. (I don't mean whiskey; I mean immunizations.) At a surface level, I don't want my kids subjected to the pain of a shot, and it certainly doesn't make me happy to put them through it. But at the root of the decision to get our kids immunized is the desire for them not to get diseases; that would make them and us unhappy. No disease equals happiness. We always do what we want, because we think it will ultimately be to our happiness.

But the problem, as I've said, isn't happiness itself, nor is it the pursuit of happiness. So, what do we do with Solomon, who pursues pleasure with all his might and then comes back and says, "Well, you can pursue it if you want, but it's meaningless. It's chasing the wind"? C. S. Lewis can help us out here. He once wrote, "I didn't go to religion to make me happy. I always knew a bottle of Port would do that."[9] And in his classic work "The Weight of Glory" he writes:

> If there lurks in most modern minds the notion that to desire our own good and earnestly to hope for the enjoyment of it is a bad thing, I submit that this notion has crept in from Kant and the Stoics and is no part of the Christian faith.[10]

Immanuel Kant was a philosopher who taught that the more you love something, the less virtuous your love becomes. (I know; it barely makes sense.) According to Kant, I would be more virtuous to hate my wife but stay with her because of my commitment to her than it would be to actually love her and love being with her. I would be more virtuous to deplore the very existence of my wife, but because of my vow, stay with her than it would be to love her with my whole heart. Kant clearly needed a hug.

But hasn't this idea infiltrated even Christianity? Don't we somehow elevate the idea of loving people even when we don't feel like it? Don't we somehow communicate that it's virtuous to perform acts of love for people we are otherwise repulsed by? But when Jesus looked out at the crowd, he didn't feel revulsion; he felt compassion (Matt. 9:36). It is true that "love is a verb" and all that, and when Paul defines love in 1 Corinthians 13, he does not do so from the framework of *feelings*, but God has not made us to experience love as a bunch of sourpusses. He gives us affections for a reason. So Lewis is dead on when he writes:

> I submit that this notion has crept in from Kant and the Stoics and is no part of the Christian faith. Indeed, if we consider the unblushing promises of reward and the staggering nature of the rewards promised in the Gospels, it would seem that Our Lord finds our desires not too strong, but too weak.[11]

According to Lewis, God doesn't look at us and say, "I can't believe they're seeking their own pleasure," but he looks at us and says, "They're not seeking hard enough." The kicker comes in Lewis's next assertion:

> We are half-hearted creatures, fooling about with drink and sex and ambition when infinite joy is offered us, like an ignorant child who wants to go on making mud pies in a slum because he cannot imagine what is meant by the offer of a holiday at the sea. We are far too easily pleased.[12]

When sin entered the world and fractured it, Romans 1:23 tells us that you and I exchanged the infinite creator God for his creation. When that took place, we began to settle for temporary fleeting pleasures rather than for what is eternal and soul-satisfying.

Ten years ago, you had in your mind a picture of what you wanted life to look like ten years later, and you thought that if you could achieve *that*, you would be happy and satisfied. For the last ten years you have put your energy—consciously or sub-consciously—into getting there. Most of you thought, "Man, if I could just get out of school, if I could get a good job, if I could find a husband (wife), if I could have children, if I could make enough money to go on vacation, if I could get a car that actually ran half the time, if I could do this, if I could get that "But the reality is, even if you've met those goals, you aren't really done, because you've already replaced that ten-year plan with a new ten-year plan. Almost all of us, whether we'll admit it or not, have bought into the philosophy that what we need to finally make us happy is more of what we already possess. This is madness. It's all meaningless.

Ecclesiastes 3:11 says that God "has put eternity into man's heart." At some level, in the deepest parts of our soul, our soul remembers, however that happens, what life was like before the fall. At some really deep level, our soul has this impression cut into it by the finger of God, like the grooves on a record, encoding the memory of what it was like before sin entered into the world. We remember, at a really deep level, that at one time we were full, and at one time we were happy, and at one time there was nothing weighing us down. Our souls are outright *groaning* to get back there. But the void is God-shaped, according to Pascal:

> There was once in man a true happiness of which there now remain to him only the mark and empty trace, which he in vain tries to fill from all his surroundings, seeking from things absent to help he does not obtain in things present. . . . But these are all inadequate, because the infinite abyss can only be filled by an infinite and immutable object, that is to say, only by God Himself.[13]

The groove is the length of eternity, and all that we have in our own power to fill it with is temporary. Solomon goes to the end of his goals and says it's all vanity, it's all meaningless, and not even the richest, wisest, most experienced man in human history possesses the resources to get there. What kind of shot do you think *you* have?

My favorite story in the Bible is in John 4. The Scriptures say that Jesus decides to go through Samaria despite the fact that nobody went through Samaria, at least not Jews. He sits down at a well, and a woman who is at the time exchanging sex for rent shows up in the middle of the day, because if she went in the morning, she'd probably get beaten up. She's a complete social outcast.

Jesus says to her, "Hey, will you get me a drink of water?" And she scoops up some water, although she's kind of freaked out that he would even talk to her. She hands him the water, and he takes a drink, and then he starts talking to her about water. He says, "You know, I'm going to drink this, but I'm going to get thirsty again." So she asks him, "Do you want another cup?" (This is a paraphrase by the way.)

He continues talking to her about water, saying, "People are going to come to this well all day long. In fact, the same women that were here this morning drawing water for the day are going to be back because they're going to be thirsty again." Then he says to her: "Listen, if you drink the water I'm offering, you will never thirst again." And she completely misses it.

Do you remember the story? She says, "You don't even have a cup. What are you talking about, 'You have water'?"

What *is* Jesus saying? He is saying, "I am eternal. I fill the void. I fit the groove."

Now, let me tell you what I'm saying and what I'm not saying. I'm not saying that, outside of Jesus, you're not going to have a good marriage. Lauren and I have good friends in our neighborhood who do not know Christ and have no desire to be church folk. We have them in our house all the time. We're just trying to let them see Jesus in us. But our neighbor is a great husband, his wife is a great wife, and they are good parents. They possess the creativity and the competence to perform their duties well, better than many Christians even! Despite all this, though, they will never know the fullness of what marriage was created to be, because only those who have submitted to Christ can experience the fullness of soul that is ultimate happiness.

In the end, there is nothing under the sun that brings lasting fulfillment. You have to look beyond the sun. The groove in our hearts cannot be filled with the temporal. It demands eternity.

Therefore, our very searching for more and more, for bigger and bigger, and for better and better, is our sense that something is off, amiss, deformed, and broken. In the same sense that death, pain, and suffering tell us that something in the world is broken, our insatiable searching tells us that something bigger than the earth itself is missing from our soul.

The Ache for Real Satisfaction

What we are attempting to establish is that sin isn't just a personal thing; it's a cosmic thing. While the gospel on the ground shows us that depravity is very personal, that it's *in here*, the gospel in the air shows us that depravity affects earth's very social fabric and systems, that it's also *out there*. Of course, it is *out there* because it's *in here*, but as Solomon's recollections in Ecclesiastes reveal, it's not just that we are in need of satisfaction, but that every good thing in the universe (apart from God) is too broken to satisfy.

How dissatisfied does this fracture leave Solomon?

> So I hated life, because what is done under the sun was grievous to me, for all is vanity and a striving after wind. I hated all my toil in which I toil under the sun, seeing that I must leave it to the man who will come after me, and who knows whether he will be wise or a fool? Yet he will be master of all for which I toiled and used my wisdom under the sun. This also is vanity. So I turned about and gave my heart up to despair over all the toil of my labors under the sun, because sometimes a person who has toiled with wisdom and knowledge and skill must leave everything to be enjoyed by someone who did not toil for it. This also is vanity and a great evil. (Eccles. 2:17–21)

There is a diminishing return on the pleasure Solomon is seeking, so he starts to hate life. He has sucked all the marrow out of it, and he's only in his thirties. He moves from being grieved to being frustrated. Notice that he's even frustrated about what will come after him. What we know from history is that, after Solomon, the nation of Israel completely dissolved. In this passage we catch him looking at his sons. He has been wise; he has built Israel to be wealthy and powerful, and he's looking at his boys and thinking, "We're in trouble. I have done nothing but manage this thing wisely, and these guys coming up behind me will destroy it." He realizes he is powerless to control what will happen to the wealth he has accumulated. He can't take it with him, and he can't make sure it won't be squandered after he's gone. The meaninglessness begins to settle in, and he gives his heart over to despair.

I'm going to horribly date myself with this example, but I was (am) a huge Nirvana fan. I paid close attention to what happened to Kurt Cobain, to what *Kurt Cobain* did to Kurt Cobain. Throughout history there have been prominent figures who, very early in life, achieved everything they could ever have dreamed of, and then they ran out of dreams. When that happens, despair takes over. I think this is what happened to Kurt Cobain. When the gnawing sense of waste began to spread in his soul, what was he going to do—make another platinum record? Was he going to buy another house, another trinket? Do you think a new cell phone would have perked him up? He entered into a despair that his favorite things—his family and his music—could no longer lift. He took his own life because, despite all he'd accomplished and achieved and accumulated, he hated life.

That is what happened to Solomon. "I have achieved it, I have done it, and I have accomplished it, and I'm going to have to leave it all to my idiot sons. It's all wasted. Man, I hate life." But pay attention to his testimony as it progresses. Hating his life is not the end of the story. He begins to ask the eternal question: "What has a man from all the toil and striving of heart with which he toils beneath the sun?" (Eccles. 2:22).

He's talking about those who get everything they want. If Job is a book about a guy who loses everything, Ecclesiastes is about a guy who gets everything. This guy feels as though the world is full of nothing but sorrow, because he's acquired everything there is to acquire, and it has only increased his sorrow. "What has a man from all the toil and striving of heart with which he toils beneath the sun? For all his days are full of sorrow, and his work is a vexation. Even in the night his heart does not rest. This also is vanity" (vv. 22–23). If every prescription the wisest man in the world can come up with doesn't work, something's not right with us or the world. Is there an answer? Is it all hopeless?

Solomon does discover the answer. He writes, "There is nothing better for a person than that he should eat and drink and find enjoyment in his toil. This also, I saw, is from the hand of God, for apart from him who can eat or who can have enjoyment?" (vv. 24–25). What Solomon has just said is that lasting enjoyment experienced by the soul is a gift from Jesus.

God gives gifts to all men. Whether you believe in God or not, you are living, walking, and wearing his stuff. He gives gifts to all: food, drink, work, friends, family. He gives gifts to all, but only the children of God, only those who believe in Jesus, receive the gift of lasting enjoyment. Why? Because if we're oriented around Jesus, our satisfaction is not tied to anything but him. We can actually enjoy God's good gifts the way they're designed to be enjoyed, because they are in orbit around the right sun—not our self, but our Savior.

The majority of human beings believe that people and circumstances exist to make them happy. We believe the brokenness inside will be satisfied by things outside. If we're not happy, who's to blame? People and circumstances. Do you see how this doesn't even make sense—broken people expecting broken people to fix them or expecting good things to do God things for them? It's a ridiculous notion, if we can think rightly about it.

The whole thing is messed up. The system and all its parts are lacking. Doesn't Ecclesiastes show us this? There is no *shalom* in our hearts, and there is no *shalom* in the offerings of the world. We are cursed; creation is cursed. We are groaning; creation is groaning. The ache is bigger than all of us.

We need a redemption bigger than all of us.

7

Reconciliation

When God surveys the depraved mess mankind has become, he notes Noah's righteousness but describes the pervasiveness of sin and the repercussions of it this way:

> Now the earth was corrupt in God's sight, and the earth was filled with violence. And God saw the earth, and behold, it was corrupt, for all flesh had corrupted their way on the earth. And God said to Noah, "I have determined to make an end of all flesh, for the earth is filled with violence through them. Behold, I will destroy them with the earth." (Gen. 6:11–13)

Why would God flood the whole earth? What did the earth ever do to God?

The answer, of course, is nothing, but the destruction of all living things—save those in the ark—shows the deep ramifications of our cosmic treason against God. Because the stewards of creation are corrupt, the earth is corrupt. We are the opposites of King Midas—everything we touch turns not to gold but to ash. The ground is accursed on account of Adam and Eve's sin, on account of *our* sin, because the consequences of sin must reflect the expanse of God's glory.

God's glory is eternal; therefore, sin is an eternal offense. This is why we believe in an eternal life, an eternal hell, and a remaking of not just some things but all things. The good news is that God's plan for redemption is scaled to his glory, encompassing all creation. What is corrupt will be declared "very good" again. At the tail end of the story of Noah and the ark, as Noah finally plants his feet on dry land again and makes a burnt offering to the Lord, God promises, "I will never again curse the ground because of man, for the intention of man's heart is evil from his youth. Neither will I ever again strike down every living creature as I have done" (Gen. 8:21).

God's promise back then is a foreshadow of that day still to come when the curse will finally be eradicated from the earth, from pole to pole and from east to west. God's plan of redemption is gigantic. The vision he has for the world, then, is not destruction, as some Christians foresee, but redemption, restoration. "For the earth will be filled with the knowledge of the glory of the LORD as the waters cover the sea," Habakkuk 2:14 tells us. We will be flooded again but this time with living water!

Clearly, the reconciliation God has in mind through the atoning work of Jesus Christ is both personal and *super*-personal. Because all things in the earth have been corrupted by man's fall, God will be "reconciling the world to himself" (2 Cor. 5:19) and putting "all things in subjection under his feet" (1 Cor. 15:27).

The Epic Work of Christ

When Jesus was teaching his disciples how to pray, his example included this petition to the Father: "Your kingdom come, your will be done, on earth as it is in heaven" (Matt. 6:10). This was in essence the purpose of his ministry: to bring the kingdom of God to bear on the earth. In heaven, all things are oriented to the worship of God. The triune Godhead is at the center of the heavenly universe. On earth, the fall has knocked everything out of orbit. We revolve around an assortment of idols, which is just a projection of our orientation around *ourselves* as gods.

As we have seen, however, the entire creation is also out of sorts this way. The stain of sin affects creation. The very ground we walk on is cursed on our account. Jesus's ministry of inaugurating God's kingdom, with himself as king, was not simply a mission of recruitment of subjects, although it is firstly and chiefly that, but it is also about reversing the curse. The Gospels show us Jesus and his friends preaching "the gospel of the kingdom," which is about God's beginning to set all things right, the ensuring that God's glory is reflected everywhere on earth just like it is in heaven. Jesus's mission, then, is both personal transformation and global transformation. His work is epic.

We see throughout Christ's ministry the foretastes of the gospel in the air. For instance, notice throughout the Gospels that Jesus redeems the souls of men and women and their history. The hopes of God's children throughout the Old Testament are not simply about individual salvation—although that is obviously in view—but about national redemption, covenantal restoration, and "real world" reconciliation.

The average Jew's expectations may have been off-center from what was realized in Jesus, but the hopes and longings we see throughout the old covenant's Law and Prophets are not ignored by God in Christ. What I mean is that the Jews of Jesus's day may have been expecting their long-awaited messiah to overthrow the Romans politically and militarily, but just because Jesus didn't do it *that way*, doesn't mean he didn't do it. When we see Jesus doing things like fulfilling the focus of the law in his Sermon on the Mount, or instituting the Lord's Supper as an ongoing fulfillment of the Passover, or violently cleansing the temple, or pronouncing woes over Jerusalem and the religious leaders, we are seeing him proclaim a kingdom restoration that is about individual transformation *and more*. He is in these acts and others, proclaiming that the gospel is the fulfillment of every nation's political, religious, cultural, and historical longing.

The gospel of Jesus is epic. When Jesus says he saw Satan fall like lightning from the sky, he is saying that the gospel is about the overthrow of evil itself, not just about our sinful behavior. When Jesus casts out demons, he is saying that the gospel is about his authority and God's sovereignty. When Jesus heals the sick and the lame, he is saying that the gospel is about the eradication of physical brokenness. When Jesus feeds the five thousand, he is saying that the gospel is about God's abundant provision through Christ to a world of hunger. When Jesus walks on water or calms the storm, he is saying that the gospel is about his lordship over the chaos of fallen creation. When Jesus confounds the religious leaders, overturns tables, tells rich people it will be hard for them, renders unto Caesar, enters the city on a jackass, predicts the temple's destruction, and stands silent before the political rulers, he is saying the gospel has profound effects on our systems. When Jesus forgives sin and raises the dead, he is saying the gospel is about individuals being born again, but he's also saying that the gospel is about his conquest of sin and death.

The mission of Jesus is so big that John the Baptist, in Matthew 3:3, wants us to remember these words from Isaiah 40:3–4:

> In the wilderness prepare the way of the LORD;
>> make straight in the desert a highway for our God.
> Every valley shall be lifted up,
>> and every mountain and hill be made low;
> the uneven ground shall become level,
>> and the rough places a plain.

Do you see that the work of Jesus is epic? It is earth-shaking. This work culminates, of course, in the end for which the Son was sent: to die on a cross and rise again.

The Cosmic Cross

Let's return to Romans 8, this time looking at it from a different vantage point.

> For I consider that the sufferings of this present time are not worth comparing with the glory that is to be revealed to us. For the creation waits with eager longing for the revealing of the sons of God. For the creation was subjected to futility, not willingly, but because of him who subjected it, in hope that the creation itself will be set free from its bondage to corruption and obtain

the freedom of the glory of the children of God. For we know that the whole creation has been groaning together in the pains of childbirth until now. And not only the creation, but we ourselves, who have the firstfruits of the Spirit, groan inwardly as we wait eagerly for adoption as sons, the redemption of our bodies. (vv. 18–23)

In our survey of creation (chapter 5), we said that Romans 8 sets a scene in *media res*, like what we see in action movies that begin with everything in chaos and falling apart before the main character begins to think about how it all began. You don't have to be religious to be able to look at the state of the world and say, "Something has gone wrong," and ask, "How did we get here?" But after the movie flashes back and reveals scene by scene the story leading up to the point of crisis, it catches back up to the present. The climax to the story is approaching, and a new question emerges: "How do we get out of this mess?"

Everyone has an answer to this question. Nearly everyone has a plan to escape from the violence. Every religion has a proposed escape route. Political candidates have plenty of ideas. Oprah has lots of suggestions for us. Half the books in the bookstore are self-help books. The need for repair is ever-pressing, and would-be repair manuals are not hard to come by.

In our look at Romans 8 this time around, you will see that Paul, even as he's revealing the brokenness, reveals the fix. He says "creation waits with eager longing," that there is a desire, that there is an expectation within creation that something is going to come that ends the wrong and puts things back together. The fracture is begging for reconciliation. Paul uses the illustration, as in 1 Thessalonians 5:3 and Galatians 4:19, of the pains of childbirth. There is anguish, but something beautiful is coming. Have you heard how the Scientologists have to be quiet when giving birth? Lauren and I took the opposite approach. She was screaming, I was screaming, and the doctor was screaming at us to quit screaming. But the baby enters the room and with it joy. Paul is trying to capture this vivid picture of the pains of childbirth to tell us that something is being birthed in this brokenness. Our bodies are groaning from brokenness and for redemption; likewise, all of creation cries out in the expectation that what went wrong will be set right. What is the fix? It is to be set free, to experience adoption, and to know redemption. And according to Romans 8 it is not just we who are crying out for this fix, but our world.

The cosmic scope of Christ's crucifixion is revealed in the events surrounding it. Recall the details of Matthew 27:45–54:

> Now from the sixth hour there was darkness over all the land until the ninth hour. And about the ninth hour Jesus cried out with a loud voice, saying, "Eli, Eli, lema sabachthani?" that is, "My God, my God, why have you forsaken me?" And some of the bystanders, hearing it, said, "This man is calling Elijah." And one of them at once ran and took a sponge, filled it with sour wine, and put it on a reed and gave it to him to drink. But the others said, "Wait, let us see whether Elijah will come to save him." And Jesus cried out again with a loud voice and yielded up his spirit. And behold, the curtain of the temple was torn in two, from top to bottom. And the earth shook, and the rocks were split. The tombs also were opened. And many bodies of the saints who had fallen asleep were raised, and coming out of the tombs after his resurrection they went into the holy city and appeared to many. When the centurion and those who were with him, keeping watch over Jesus, saw the earthquake and what took place, they were filled with awe and said, "Truly this was the Son of God!"

The sky grows dark. The earth shakes. The temple veil is torn in two. Graves pop open, and resurrected bodies are doing the "Thriller" dance down the streets of Jerusalem. Clearly, what Christ is enacting on the cross is bigger than our puny minds can fathom. The reaction of the natural order connects Christ's death to a rift in the fabric of creation itself.

Romans 8, which gives us that dual perspective of the consequences of the fall—the groaning on the ground and in the air—points to the cross as the means of being set free to the freedom of the glory. We receive this double vision in Colossians 1, as well. In that passage, Paul clearly talks about the nature of the gospel in regard to individuals. You and I as individuals are reconciled to God by Jesus Christ—specifically, by the cross and resurrection of Jesus Christ, not by any work of our own:

> And you, who once were alienated and hostile in mind, doing evil deeds, he has now reconciled in his body of flesh by his death, in order to present you holy and blameless and above reproach before him. (vv. 21–22)

We are reconciled to God by the crucifixion and resurrection of Jesus Christ, and Colossians speaks of that truth often: "He has delivered us from the domain of darkness and transferred us to the kingdom of his beloved Son" (1:13). Reconciled by Christ, we're no longer enemies with God. The personal relationship that Adam and Eve enjoyed with him has been restored. But Colossians 1 also gives us a wide-angle view, from high above, of this restoration. It's like zooming in on your house on GoogleEarth, and then scanning back out to look at the western hemisphere.

Of Christ Paul writes:

> He is the image of the invisible God, the firstborn of all creation. For by him all things were created, in heaven and on earth, visible and invisible, whether thrones or dominions or rulers or authorities—all things were created through him and for him. And he is before all things, and in him all things hold together. (Col. 1:15–17)

This is cosmic, is it not? This is not you sitting on Jesus's lap; it is not individualized. This is unbelievably cosmic. He is the creator of all things. He is the sustainer of all things. "In him all things hold together." Everything is by Christ, through Christ, and for Christ, from human beings to elephants, from bioluminescent fish in some black cave in South America no person's ever discovered to microbes underneath a glacier on some distant planet no person ever will. Christ is Lord over it all. Colossians 1 wants us to see Christ's lordship as very, very *big*. He is certainly not less than our personal Lord and savior, but he is certainly fathoms, light-years, and eons *more* than that.

Paul continues:

> And he is the head of the body, the church. He is the beginning, the firstborn from the dead, that in everything he might be preeminent. For in him all the fullness of God was pleased to dwell, and through him to reconcile to himself all things, whether on earth or in heaven, making peace by the blood of his cross. (vv. 18–20)

One of the dangers of a gospel that stays on the ground too long is man-centeredness. The idea, for instance, that "the Bible is God's love letter to you" has a kernel of truth to it, but it is illustrative of how easily we trade the centrality of God's glory for the centrality of our need. Colossians 1:18 is a dagger in the heart of the man-centered gospel. Christ is the head; Christ is the beginning; Christ is the firstborn; Christ must be preeminent. The explicit gospel, then, magnifies God's glory as it heralds the supremacy of his Son. The gospel of Colossians 1 is epic; it posits a cross that is cosmic. We see that the peace that is made by the blood of the cross covers "all things."[1] The scope of Christ's reconciling work on the cross spans the brokenness between man and God *and* the brokenness between earth and heaven.

The cross of Christ is first and centrally God's means of reconciling sinful people to his sinless self. But it is bigger than that too. From the ground we see the cross as our bridge to God. From the air, the cross is our bridge to the restoration of all things. The cross of the battered Son of God is the battering ram through the blockade into Eden. It is our key into a *better* Eden, into the wonders of the new-covenant kingdom, of which the old was just a shadow.

The cross is the linchpin in God's plan to restore all creation. Is it any wonder, then, that the empty tomb opened out into a garden?

Reconciled to Reconcile

For the reconciliation enacted by the cross to be cosmic, then, it must encompass more than just our individual relationship with God. We each may be saved as an individual life, but we are not saved *to* an individual life. We stand as part of God's restoring of all things, and we are brought into the missional witness to God's restorative gospel, the body of Christ.

When you and I are reconciled by Jesus Christ to God, we are brought into the covenant community of faith. We are brought into the church universal. We are members of, as the Scriptures call us, "the body of Christ." At the universal level, I have brothers and sisters all over the world. I have been in Jaipur, India, where they worship Jesus in Hindi. I've been to China, Africa, and Mexico, where people don't look or talk like most of us in America, but, in Christ, we have family there. We are saved into the family of God at the universal level, so we've got brothers and sisters all over the world. In almost every tribe, tongue, and nation on earth, there are those who say, "Jesus is Lord."

In Christ, we've also been called not just into the church universal but to the church local. In my case, I am the pastor of The Village Church in Dallas, which means I am in a covenant relationship with the other members of The Village Church. I am called to them, and they are called to me. I am a part of them, and they are a part of me. Their gifts and my gifts collide in a community of faith so that we all become all that God would have for us to be together in Christ.

All of this means that I am not adequate in and of myself to pull this "body of Christ" thing off, and you are not adequate in and of yourself to pull it off either. We've been given the covenant community because we need each other, and together we'll be more mature, experience more life, and know more joy than we ever would apart from one another.

This is a drum that the New Testament never stops beating. We are to outdo one another in honor (Rom. 12:10), we are to serve one another (Gal. 5:13; 1 Pet. 4:10), and we are to be built up by what every joint supplies (Eph. 4:15–16). God has intrinsically wired and gifted you as an individual, and that wiring and gifting has not been given to you simply for your own purposes but rather for the building up of the body of Christ into maturity.

Thinking about gospel reconciliation in concentric circles, we are reconciled first to God in Christ, then to one another in covenant community, and third to what God is doing in the renewal of all creation.[2] To put it another way, think of the gospel as a stone landing in a pond. The life, death, and resurrection of Jesus are the cause of many ripples; they are the epicenter of God's work in the world. The first ripple is our personal reconciliation to God. The second ripple establishes the body of Christ, as we are reconciled to each other. The third ripple is the missional posture of the church as we mobilize to proclaim the fullness of reconciliation in the gospel. In essence, we are reconciled to reconcile.

Paul calls this missional work the "ministry of reconciliation," which he tracks in 2 Corinthians 5:17–20:

> Therefore, if anyone is in Christ, he is a new creation. The old has passed away; behold, the new has come. All this is from God, who through Christ reconciled us to himself and gave us the ministry of reconciliation; that is, in Christ God was reconciling the world to himself, not counting their trespasses against them, and entrusting to us the message of reconciliation. Therefore, we are ambassadors for Christ, God making his appeal through us. We implore you on behalf of Christ, be reconciled to God.

Notice how he starts with individual transformation, highlighting the work of the gospel on the ground: "If anyone is in Christ, he is a new creation." Then he progresses from singular to plural: God "through Christ reconciled *us*." Then he progresses from our reconciliation together to God to our outward work of sharing the gospel: God "gave us the ministry of reconciliation." In this one passage we see that we are reconciled as individuals, but this is not the end of the gospel story or its implications. We are given the gift of trusting Christ, then entrusted with repeating the message of this gift.

Missional Mind-Sets

The explicit gospel transforms the way we conceive of the mission of the church. If the gospel is cosmic as well as personal, the Great Commission joins us to God's mission to restore all things. This means the ministry of reconciliation is bigger and more multifaceted than many of us envision.

To be very clear, however, the mission of the church can be put very simply. The mission of the church is essentially evangelism and discipleship. But how we carry out those efforts really matters. How do we disciple and how do we evangelize? There are, generally speaking, two primary modes of doing the work of mission. One mode we might call *attractional*. The other we might call *incarnational*, or *missional*.[3]

When it comes to evangelism, some people simply come to church and hear about the gospel there. Their neighbors don't necessarily share the gospel with them personally, but they'll say, "Hey, you really ought to come to church with me. You ought to hear my pastor speak." Or they'll say, "Hey, come to my small group with me. Sit in here and listen." So we bring them to a place where the gospel is being taught or presented. We can call this approach to evangelism "attractional" because it is about attracting people to a gospel presentation rather than taking the gospel presentation to them. We might say it recasts "Go and tell" as "Come and hear."

In this model, if faith takes root, if God opens eyes, if God opens hearts and people say, "I put my faith in Christ," then the process of discipleship begins. The Great Commission, after all, is "Go and make disciples," not "Go make converts." (This is an imperative point to understand. Some churches have become massive because, in the end, no one is interested in discipleship but in accumulating decisions passed off as conversions. And that is chasing the wind. It's a level of foolishness that helps nobody and does nothing in regard to the mandate that we've been given to be agents of reconciliation in a world that is longing for freedom from the bondage of decay.) In the end, discipleship occurs in the church, usually either organically or mechanically.

Let me explain the difference. I was part of a group of pastors several years ago that had a leadership network called Think Group. They took about fifteen pastors who were thirty-five years old and under with churches of two thousand or less and put us all in a room together to talk. Then they brought in older pastors to mentor us, to talk about how they did things in their churches, how they designed systems and pastored their people. The first issue we all wanted to talk about was discipleship. "How do people mature in their faith, and what's the role of the church in that? How do you design it?" Think Group brought in two guys who were polar opposites. The first guy said, "We want to Velcro people to the Bible and to others." I wasn't sure exactly what he meant, and because I'm a bit of a pragmatist, I asked: "Does it work?"

He said, "Well, we've got X number of people in groups, and we have X number of people in this group and that program . . ."

The problem, though, is that getting people into groups doesn't necessarily mean they're being discipled. It doesn't mean they're maturing in their faith. And I know from experience that it's possible to have a lot of people in a lot of groups and still not have many people maturing in their faith.

The other guy was the polar opposite. Where the first guy was promoting a more organic, home-based approach to discipleship, sort of banking on maturity happening naturally, the other guy proposed a more mechanical, one-size-fits-all approach to assimilating people into a discipleship system. He had three volumes of material to share with us. His church had a two-year program that one had to go through to learn leadership, theology, philosophy, and all kinds of other things. It sounded sort of like seminary classes for Average Joes. My question was the same: "Is it working?"

"Oh yeah," he said. "It has been great."

So my second question was, "How many people have you taken through this program?"

"Thirteen," he said.

That was out of around four thousand people. And, let me tell you, thirteen people trained that way is a gift! If you look at the model of Jesus's ministry, he had only eleven. So in some sense, there's something good about having thirteen. But in regard to just lay-level discipleship, it doesn't seem as efficient as it aims to be. His approach reminded me a lot of Greek classes. If you haven't taken Greek, let me tell you what it looks like. There are a lot of people in class the first day, but by the time you're done, only a remnant is left. It's like a brotherhood. That's why those who have actually completed their Greek studies deserve tremendous respect. If you've seen guys who fought in a war together, they've got a camaraderie built around the rigor and the risk they shared. They stuck their necks out together. This is very similar to people who have survived learning Koine Greek. It starts big, and it just dwindles down to a small brotherhood of survivors.

All of that is to say that, in the end, the mechanical type of discipleship has a glaring weakness. You can get a lot of people into the front door, but only a few make it to the end. I could easily stand up at The Village Church and say, "This is how we're doing discipleship. These are the classes we're doing. You need to sign up for these classes. You can get to first base, second base, and third base, and then you'll be discipled." What would happen is everyone would sign up, and attendance the first couple of weeks would be stellar. Then it would just dwindle and dwindle and dwindle. It's one of the weaknesses of the mechanical model.

But there are weaknesses to the organic model, as well. It's hard to know what's going on in relationships, how to accurately gauge if maturity is being cultivated. The mechanical approach may be too black-and-white, but organic is too gray.

One of the things we've tried to do at The Village is what we call the "green house." We're trying to do mechanical with organic simultaneously. We want people to learn, know, and understand doctrine and theology, but we want them to do that within the context of relationships. We have found that acquiring information outside of rooted relationships turns immature Christians into the theology police. And nobody likes the theology police. When that sort of doctrinal arrogance takes over, people end up despising doctrine because they can't see the beauty of it from the beauty of reconciled relationships. We just see what Paul calls, in 1 Corinthians 13:1, "a clanging cymbal." We want that organic, relational connection thing happening, but we also need some structure so people know how to join, and people know what they're supposed to learn.

But all of that is predicated on the attractional mode of mission. People come to the church and get converted, and then we begin to disciple them. There's nothing intrinsically wrong with an attractional approach done in a biblically appropriate way. It's not wrong to invite people to church or a small group. We *should* do that. Attractional mangles mission only when it's the *only* mode at work.

The *incarnational* mode of ministry, on the other hand, reminds us that discipleship and evangelism shouldn't be taking place simply within the church walls but also outside the church walls. The incarnational approach tries to break down the wall of sacred/secular so we can begin to see everything as sacred and quit being so fearful of the secular.

There are, according to sociologists, seven domains of society: economics, agriculture, education, medicine, science and technology, communications, arts and entertainment, governance and justice, and family. In the incarnational mode of ministry, the church's mission of evangelism and discipleship has us intentionally living in these seven domains as agents of gospel reconciliation. So when we look at our jobs, for instance, no matter what our job is, we view it not as our purpose in life but rather as where God has sovereignly placed us for the purpose of making Christ known and his name great. If you are a teacher, if you are a politician, if you are a businessman, if you are in agriculture, if you are in construction, if you are in technology, if you are in the arts, then you should not be saying, "I need to find my life's purpose in this work," but rather, "I need to bring God's purpose to this work." The missional Christian should see all things through the lens of the gospel, because the gospel's aim is "all things."

To extrapolate from this, the missional mind-set has implications for what we would call "ministries of mercy" or "social ministries." When we begin to receive God's heart for "all things," we begin to live open-handed. We live beneath our means so that we can bless those who have less than we do. We go into other parts of the world to care for the "least of these" (Matt. 25:34–40). It's why we want to meet with city officials and ask them, "What can we do to help this city? How can our church be a place that's *for* the city?" This is a natural result of being reconciled to God and to one another and then, as agents of reconciliation, engaging the world around us.

Now, there are two major errors we can fall into in these efforts. There are land mines we have to be careful not to step on, and they bring quite a lot of controversy among pastors' ranks. Land mine number-one is building all of our acts of mercy, all our acts of social justice, around a contingent evangelism. Evangelism is necessary, of course, but what I mean by a "contingent evangelism" is what happens when churches do that "We've got food for you if you're a believer" sort of thing. Some say, "We've got resources for you if you believe." Or, "You can receive our help if you indicate a decision for Christ." There may be a few situations where this contingency makes sense, but it is largely manipulative. It's a legalistic bait-and-switch, and that is not reflective of the heart of God toward man.

We are to freely love the alien and the stranger, because we were aliens and strangers, and God loved us. We had no hope, and he gave us hope. The reconciling gospel is always at the forefront of the church's social action, because a full belly is not better than a reconciled soul. One is temporary; one is eternal. If we don't have silver and gold, "such as we have" (see Acts 3:6 KJV) is still eternally priceless. *But this doesn't mean we don't fill the belly.* We fill the belly. We live open-handed lives and seek to spot injustice and despair around us, and we enter into sorrow and pain so that the love, mercy, and beauty of God's reconciling work in Christ can be seen in our lives in the hopes that a broken world will see and give praise to God.

In the end, James is clear that to truly understand the gospel is to be transformed in how you live, specifically in these areas of justice and mercy for the sick, the hungry, the poor, and the marginalized. If the gospel does indeed have profound ramifications for "all things," we should expect our mission to have implications for cultures, systems, and structures. So the first land mine in missional effort is assuming wrongly that works of love and mercy must be contingent on evangelistic response.

If the first land mine is establishing an inappropriate evangelistic contingency, land mine number-two is removing the atoning work of Jesus Christ from missional action altogether. The essential problem of all mankind is not a lack of resources but a lack of holiness. Some Christians seem to think that the cross of Christ for the forgiveness of sins is an optional component to Christian mission. Yet, if we jettison the cross, not only do we lose our mission, we also lose our ability to authentically call what we're doing "Christian."

As a guy who pastors a church of predominantly upper-middle-class people, I can tell you that having clean water and living in nice houses does not fix the root of what's wrong with mankind. There is just as much darkness and despair where there's access to indoor plumbing and excellent medical care as there is in places that don't have those things. I know some people will get really angry when they hear that. But I've been in both kinds of places. There are three miles of paved road in southern Sudan. And if there's any clean water, it's via a pump. Is there loss there? Absolutely. Is there despair there? Absolutely. Is there hope there? Oddly enough, there's frequently more hope there than I see in Dallas, Texas, sometimes. But in the end, classic liberalism would say, "Hey, let's get rid of this whole 'sin' thing and let's not say too much about the atoning work of Jesus Christ, because then more people can get on board with feeding the hungry, taking care of the poor, reaching out to the marginalized, and working against injustice. People will be more inclined to rally around that." This sort of drift would change us from Christian missionaries to charitable do-gooders, which is something any heretic can be.

The single most loving act we can do is share the good news of Jesus Christ, that God saves sinners. The singular problem of humanity is not material lack or physical deficiency—it is personal sin against a holy God. It is this problem, in fact, that has created the attendant problems of material lack and physical deficiency in the first place. We are so shortsighted sometimes that we miss the complexity that results from the simple gospel. It is the gospel on the ground that opens up restoration for the problems we see from the air. If God opens the heart and soul, the gospel begins to solve the complexities of all the systemic issues that keep people in poverty and rip countries apart.

Something that has always bothered me is how many kids in third-world countries die of diarrhea. You and I could go right now to a gas station and buy medicine that would save the lives of hundreds of thousands of children in lands just a plane ride from here. But do you know why we can't get that medicine into their hands? We can't because of the greed of men, lust for power, and political ambition. Now, these are systemic issues that the simple gospel comes in and unravels. Only the gospel can change the hearts of those holding back access to medication. Cycles of violence such as we've seen in Rwanda and witnessed in Sudan get interrupted not by ordinary acts of charity but by the gospel. Missionaries step into those situations and say, "You don't need to get revenge. You need to forgive your brother. You need to leave vengeance to God and trust him for grace. You don't need to take matters into your own hands. If God has saved you, respond in kind to those who have hurt you."

Missional power comes not from our good intentions but from the gospel itself. This knowledge demands missional humility. We can't transform. Only God does that. We're not what makes anything new. It's not our act that renews the city. It's the cross that enacts renewal. We are called simply to obey God's call, and if the gospel has "all things" in view, it is contrary to the missional mind-set to cordon some areas off as "gospel-proof." According to Abraham Kuyper, "There is not a square inch in the whole domain of our human existence over which Christ, who is sovereign over *all*, does not cry: 'Mine!'"[4] Therefore, there should be no square inch in the whole domain of human existence over which we don't say, "His!" Seeing the gospel from the air helps us keep this "whole domain" and its multitude of square inches in view. This is the missional mind-set: believing and living as if God's reconciling work is true in every space we find ourselves in.

When the gospel takes hold, it turns a Christian outward, which means it turns a church outward. We are reconciled to reconcile, and all things the church does are in service of this mission of gospel proclamation. A missional church can employ an appropriate mix of attractional and incarnational approaches to evangelism and discipleship, so long as all things are done to God's glory, not ours, and have the gospel of Jesus at their center. In Colossians 1:6, Paul says the gospel that has come among us is bearing fruit in the whole world and growing. If our hearts are tuned to the explicit gospel, then, we will be joining God in this cosmic work.

The Winning Offensive

To give you one more little picture of the cosmic level of reconciliation, let's look at Peter. I love that Peter is a disciple, because if Peter can be a disciple, anybody can be a disciple. He's just a guy who was constantly confused and trying to figure things out, and constantly speaking before he thought. This gives me a lot of hope.

In the Scriptures, we encounter a great little scene in which Jesus asks the disciples, "Hey, what's the word on the street? Who do people say that I am?" (see Matt. 16:13–20). They say, "Here's what we're hearing in the market. Some say you're Elijah; some say you're John the Baptist. Others say this; others say that." And then he asks, "Who do *you* say that I am?"

Of course the boys fall silent except for good ol' Peter. He fires off, "Well, you're the Son of God. You're the Messiah. You're the Holy One."

Jesus says, "Blessed are you, Simon, for God has revealed this to you, not man, and upon this rock, I will build my church."

Scholars offer a lot of conjecture about whether Jesus was pointing to himself as the rock or to Peter. But it's the next line that I think is most pressing for our current discussion. Jesus says, "The gates of hell won't prevail." This verse (v. 18) has huge implications for the missional posture of Christianity. Gates are not an offensive weapon, are they? Nobody says, "Let's get 'em! Put up the gate!" Nobody does that. Gates are defensive by design. So when Jesus says, "I'm going to build the church, and the gates of hell won't prevail against it," we are being told that evangelism, discipleship, justice, social aid, the engaging of God's people with his plan to renew creation—all of that and more, done in the power of the gospel—slam into the gates of hell. All we see in Romans 8 that's gone wrong is assailed by God's gospel offensive. God's plan is to renew and remake, and *God does not lose*. The gates of hell will not prevail. The missional offensive is the winning offensive. It's the *only* winning offensive.

So the fundamental posture of Christianity cannot be defense.

Do we need watchmen on the walls? Of course. Do we need people who can guard the church against heresy? Absolutely. Do we need intellectual people with compelling voices to provide strong apologetic defenses for the Christian faith? No doubt about it. But the fundamental position, the essential posture of Christ's church and of our gospel-captured lives, is one of offense, of mission.

We should not be afraid, then, to say to each other, "Let's look hard at the city, let's work for the welfare of the city, and let's identify those strongholds in and around our city and be God's agents of reconciliation in those areas." A good grasp of the gospel from the air helps us do this well.

Now, please hear what I'm saying. I don't think we can build a ladder to heaven. I'm not talking about some kind of utopia here, reached by social progression, or spiritual evolution, or what have you. No, in fact, the ladder we need has already been built—it's Jacob's ladder, and by it God is coming down; we do not go up. In the end, our responsibility is not to make our culture, our cities, our towns, or our environments into little bastions of Christian culture but rather to engage and engage and engage until God calls us home or cracks open the sky and makes all things new in an instant. But we nevertheless work to that end until he comes. Let's not be caught napping.

We go on the offensive full of gospel confidence, because we see that day coming when what God has inaugurated in Christ he finishes in Christ. We forge ahead in faith, in hope, and in love because that day of consummation is coming soon.

8

Consummation

I have a confession to make. Until recently, I mostly stayed away from end-times stuff (eschatology) and had never really preached an outright message on the consummation of all things. There are a couple of reasons for this neglect, neither of which is really an excuse, but they are reasons for which I think most readers will have understanding and sympathy. The first is that people get really weird when it comes to eschatology. The subject arouses a whole lot of passion built around conjecture.

I had some unpleasant experiences with this kind of passion early in my walk with the Lord, and it just left a bad taste in my mouth. From the guy who handed me a scroll he made in his garage during my first week as a pastor, to the wild-eyed guy on the street corner with a sandwich board sign reading "The end is near," to the fringe preachers who say we can unlock the code in the Bible to reveal the exact day of the Lord's return, I have been influenced to just avoid the topic altogether because it seems like a magnet for misfocused energy and unhinged passion. Again, I'm not saying this is a good reason not to have preached on eschatology, but it is an understandable one.

The second reason is that the Scriptures seem to me a bit confusing on this subject. I find the hermeneutic needed for apocalyptic and prophetic texts to be strange. This probably reveals my lack of formal education, but as I studied the Scriptures and read books on eschatology, I grew unsure instead of sure. I couldn't get past reading the prophecies of Isaiah as needing to be meaningful to Isaiah's day, and the prophecies in Daniel needing to mean something to Daniel. In the book of Revelation things get really strange. There are dragons, virgins, babies being eaten by dragons, a third of the earth being wiped out, stars falling from the sky, and a lot of confusion, and I have not been helped much at all by even smart men's conjecture. I got a little tired of the guessing game of whether the locust in one passage is an Apache helicopter and Gog refers to Russia.

I often found myself in the apocalyptic texts without an exegetical anchor. I would read the view of one interpretative grid and think, "Yeah, I can kind of see how that works." But then I would read another view and think, "Okay, I can kind of see this view making sense too." So when it came to eschatology, I found myself in a great deal of discomfort—not the good discomfort of God's revealing my sin but more the discomfort of not feeling confident enough in my understanding to actually proclaim it.

But two things have happened that have pushed me into a less tenuous position on this subject, prompting me to get serious about getting to the bottom of what the Bible teaches concerning the consummation of all things. The first thing was that I was diagnosed with brain cancer. I didn't tend to think a whole lot about heaven (and what comes after heaven) when I was in my twenties and early thirties, because I was in great health and never really got sick. I thought a lot about the gospel, proclaiming and preaching the gospel, knowing that the return of Christ could come at any moment and death could come at any point. I thought about these things the way a lot of us do: I was aware that I could die, and I was aware that people were going to get cancer, but I wasn't intimately aware that one of those people could be me. I knew *other* people got cancer; I didn't think it was going to be *me* that got cancer.

This is an arrogant position, but it was the position I was walking in. It's amazing how quickly your interest gets piqued to look more into eternal things when you hear "anaplastic oligodendroglioma, grade 3." That was my first kick in the pants to really examine what the Bible teaches about the future.

The second thing that happened to increase my interest in eschatology was when a friend of mine pulled me aside and told me that he thought my problem with eschatology was the result of getting bogged down in peripheral details. His rebuke was gentle but firm as he informed me that I was missing the point of studying the end times. He asked me simply, "When God finally makes all things new as he promises throughout the Scriptures, what will things look like? Where will we be?" He told me to set about answering the big questions first, and once I had a good grasp of God's plan from the cosmic level, then I could work on the details of timing and spacing, what to do with the millennium and the rest.

He was right. I had lost interest in the forest because I kept getting frustrated trying to figure out the science of the cells in two or three different trees. This is the major malfunction of so much eschatological speculation today, as well. The Bible would have us look forward to our destination and think about the wonders of that city to come, but so many evangelical prognosticators have us caught up pondering the species of grass off the exit ramp.

In the big picture presented in the gospel in the air, however, we are able to approach the subject of the end times with joy and wonder, with great expectation and hope, because we better glimpse the grandeur of God's plan for the cosmos (rather than speculating about his plan for Libya and the like). So far in our survey we've looked at how God created the universe, how our universe was fractured because of the fall of man, and how God through Christ's atoning work is reconciling all things to himself. Now we want to spend some time looking at what happens when Christ consummates what he inaugurates. What happens when God makes all things new?

The Importance of Consummation

In his book *The Bible and the Future*, Anthony Hoekema writes that it's important to understand the consummation of all things for three reasons. The first reason it's important to understand the

consummation, Hoekema says, is that we need a proper understanding of what the life to come is all about. It has been my
observation as a pastor, and as someone who travels and speaks
to a great many people, that most of us believe that, when we die,
we go to *Tom and Jerry* heaven. If you've ever watched *Tom and
Jerry* cartoons, you probably know what I'm talking about. In the
cartoon, when Tom dies, he floats up to an ethereal space among
the clouds, and there they play harps. This image, as laughable
as it is boring, is unfortunately the kind of picture most people
have of heaven. They assume that we go to heaven to play cham-
ber music while dressed in white robes, perched on a cloud or
overlooking streets of literal gold beside a literally crystal sea. We
believe this because we have been taught that the biblical symbols
teach it. We have seen many artistic renderings of this place. We
even sing songs about how heaven is going to be all about singing songs. Perhaps the most famous hymn in history includes the
words:

> When we've been there ten thousand years
> Bright shining as the sun
> We've no less days to sing God's praise
> Than when we first begun.[1]

The picture painted by this great hymn is of an eternal ses-
sion of praise music. I remember being a bit mortified by this idea
after my conversion. Although I loved the Lord, the concept of
just singing to the Lord for trillions of years was more than my
mind could fathom. I thought, "Surely we'd get bored with that."
Even the most amazing things on earth get a little boring after a
while. So how is it that billions of trillions of years from now, I'm
still going to be plucking my harp, sitting on my cloud in perfect
contentment? We forecast this future in other songs too. "In man-
sions of glory and endless delight, I'll ever adore Thee in heaven so
bright."[2] Once again, the image is conjured of robe-wearing, harp-
playing, eternal song-singing *Tom and Jerry* heaven. Is that really

what heaven will be like? Anthony Hoekema is going to say that, to understand what's actually going to occur, we need to dig in to find out what life is going to be like when all is said and done.

The second reason he says it's important to understand the consummation of all things is that we need to grasp the full dimension of God's redemptive plan. Hoekema writes:

> The total work of Christ is nothing less than to redeem this entire creation from the effects of sin. That purpose will not be accomplished until God has ushered in the new earth, until Paradise Lost has become Paradise Regained. We need a clear understanding of the doctrine of the new earth, therefore, in order to see God's redemptive program in cosmic dimensions. We need to realize that God will not be satisfied until the entire universe has been purged of all the results of man's fall.[3]

Finally, Hoekema's third reason for understanding the consummation of all things is so that we can properly understand Old Testament prophecy. The Old Testament prophecies speak of a glorious future for the earth. These prophecies tell us that, at some point in the future, the earth will become far more productive and spectacular than it is now.

For these reasons and more, I am compelled to press more fully into what the Scriptures reveal about God's plan for the future of the cosmos. Let's see what heavenly picture God's Word paints for us.

The New Heavens and the New Earth

During my first year in college, my roommate Jimmy asked me a question as I was drifting off to sleep. It was night. We were in our beds in the dorm room, and I was just at that point of losing consciousness, teetering off the threshold into sleep. That's when Jimmy said, "Hey, Matt, where in the Bible does it say we go to heaven when we die?" I was jolted awake. Now, at that moment I knew a few verses, but, by and large, I simply believed that, when I died, I was going to heaven and then someday God would destroy the earth and bring everyone still alive to heaven to be there with us. This belief was reinforced by the wildly popular *Left Behind* book series and my general ignorance of any other viewpoints on what the Scriptures had to say about this stuff. I look back to that night Jimmy's question startled me awake as the moment I realized I needed more Bible in my view of the afterlife, and since I've repented of my neglect of studying these things, I've realized that the view I was taught early on isn't totally faithful to the story in Scripture.

I can point to four things I've seen in the Scriptures that have helped change my mind in regard to the idea that God will destroy the earth and bring all of us floating up to be with him in *Tom and Jerry* heaven.

The first thing we should see is that the Old Testament views future redemption as a restoration of life in creation. It's an amazing thing to read through the Scripture's story of God's choosing a people for himself and then teaching those people and entrusting to them his plan, not just for them but for all creation. God calls Israel out of the pagan tribes and nations around them and uses them to show the world how he intends the world to work. It's important to see that the laws God gave the Israelites shaped every part of their lives. The law was meant to govern their environment, their economy, their family, their society, their politics, their personal lives, and everything between the cracks. And as Israel submitted to the laws of God, they would show the nations around them how God intended the world to function, how he intended creation and all components therein to work. Israel was going to show the world how walking as God's image bearers under explicit acknowledgment of God's sovereignty and majesty and in complete rhythm with God's design *worked*.

For those of you who know your Bible fairly well: How did the Israelites do? How well did they pull this off? I'm sure you know they stunk at it. The Old Testament chronicles their perfecting the art of failure. As they failed time and time again, the prophets among them looked forward to the day when Israel, God's chosen people, would return to their land and repent of their sin and live according to God's will. In this way, Israel was meant to be a light to the nations. The prophets would talk, often at great length, about all nations being drawn into God's kingdom so that it would encompass the whole earth. Escape from earth doesn't seem to be all that great a concern.

If you read through the entire Old Testament, you'll find that it views the destiny of humanity as inseparably linked with life on earth. Jesus himself affirms this Old Testament view of salvation. His announcement of the arrival of God's kingdom must be placed in this context. When Jesus preaches the gospel of the kingdom, the first-century Jews are hearing that the restoration of all things is at hand and that they, and those who've died righteous before them, are going to participate in this restoration and resurrection.

Jesus wasn't trying to change their understanding of a new earth and a new heaven, made perfect by God's reconciling of all things back to himself. The gospel ministry of Jesus and his followers shows Jesus operating in the framework of an Old Testament expectation of a new creation. His miraculous deeds demonstrate his healing of a broken world, revealing that the gospel of the kingdom includes the eradication of disease, the usurping of death, and the ushering in of the new order.

I'm not trying to promise more than the Bible promises here. Jesus inaugurated the kingdom in his first coming, but he hasn't consummated it yet. You and I live today in the tension of this already–not yet world where Jesus has purchased for us reconciliation, but the consummation still lies ahead. In fact, we see, in Matthew 19:28, that Jesus talks about his return bringing into being this new world. On this side of Jesus's death, resurrection, and ascension we live in the tension of the new world being paid for but not completely rolled out.

On top of this being the Old Testament understanding and its reinforcement by Jesus, Paul's understanding is also interconnected with the Old Testament's forecast of a new creation and Jesus's affirmation of this vision. We have looked at Romans 8 quite a bit so far, but there's no danger of wearing it out, so, if we look again, we see Paul, in verses 19–22, holding that even the nonhuman creation shares in the destiny of God's chosen people. The ground is cursed because of us. It groans. It has been subjected to futility. This is not to say that the earth is alive in any pantheistic, paganistic sense but only that Paul's metaphorical language here refers to the reality that the earth's brokenness is bound up with our sin, and therefore the solution to the earth's problems is bound up with our redemption.

At the time of this writing, the world has turned its gaze to Japan, where an earthquake rating 8.9 on the Richter scale and its ensuing tsunami have decimated hundreds of square miles and killed thousands of people. This tragedy is just the latest reminder that something is very wrong. What has happened in Japan, like what happens every day in places where weather kills the unprotected, children die of malaria, doctors diagnose patients with cancer, and the vanity of vanities cycles through, prompts us to groan for deliverance. All creation eagerly awaits its liberation. The liberation that you and I are going to enjoy in our new bodies, the nonhuman creation is going to enjoy in its restoration.

The goal of redemptive history is a resurrected body on a new earth. The prophet writes, "For behold, I create new heavens and a new earth, and the former things shall not be remembered or come into mind" (Isa. 65:17). I love this verse, because, as a pastor, I see firsthand horrible things happen in the lives of people. In my ministry we have buried children, young men, and young women. We have seen cancer ravage strong bodies. I've seen marriages break up because of affairs and cold-heartedness. I've heard heinous sins confessed. But Isaiah prompts me to look forward and envision the day that God will create a new heaven and a new earth, and all the former things—all the pain, sorrow, difficulty, and rebellion—will no longer be remembered at all. John tells us:

Then I saw a new heaven and a new earth, for the first heaven and the first earth had passed away, and the sea was no more. And I saw the holy city, new Jerusalem, coming down out of heaven from God, prepared as a bride adorned for her husband. (Rev. 21:1–2)

We see in these texts that the goal of redemptive history is the restoration of fallen creation through the ushering in of a new heaven and a new earth. But here's something worth noting. In Revelation 21—and in 2 Peter 3, which we will look at below—the Greek word for "new" is *kainos*, not *neos*. Now, *kainos* means "new in nature or in quality," while *neos* means "new in time or origin." In other words, when these passages employ the phrase "new heaven and new earth," they are positing a world *renewed*, not a world brand-new. Therefore, what we see in the Scripture's vision of the end of redemptive history is not an earth thrown in the trash can with its righteous inhabitants escaping to disembodied bliss in the clouds but a restored earth where creation has been reconciled to God. Looking carefully at Revelation 21, we see heaven meeting the new earth; heaven and earth collide into what is new (or renewed), and all things are made new on that new earth. What will that be like?

Lauren and I have been to Southern California multiple times. We eat at a place in La Jolla called George's on the Cove. If you're there at sunset, you can see the spectacular view of the sun setting over the Pacific Ocean. As breathtaking as that view is, we know, according to the Bible, that it is broken. It is not what it was meant to be, and as beautiful as it is, as a part of this broken world, it is only a pale imitation of the sunsets that once were and the sunsets that one day will be. Can you imagine how amazing the sunsets will be over a restored earth? I don't know if we can. Such a thought is beyond us, this side of heaven.

The Bible tells us some wondrous things about the new earth. Isaiah 35:1 tells us that the deserts shall blossom as the rose. So when we think of the desert, we think of dead wasteland, but the

Bible says that, in the new earth, the deserts are going to bloom like roses. Amos 9:13 says that the plowman shall overtake the reaper and that the mountains shall drop sweet wine. The mountains this side of consummation are spectacular, and they provoke awe, but we look forward to the new earth's mountain ranges, where fruitless rocks and frigid snow will put forth abundance and produce sweet wine. In Isaiah 65, we learn that there will be no more sounds of weeping heard on the earth, that the days of God's people shall be like the days of the tree and that on the earth the wolf and the lamb shall feed together. We see in Isaiah 11 that no one will hurt or destroy anything in all of God's holy mountain. And, according to Habakkuk 2:14, this is true because evil will be vanquished to the lake of fire, and the earth will be filled with the knowledge of the Lord as waters cover the sea.

Think of this! Slow down and ponder it. If you know somewhere in the world that is renowned for its spectacular views, what you see is nevertheless broken, and what is to come in the new earth is far beyond what you can fathom or imagine. The work that God does in us through the power of the gospel of Jesus's redemptive work is a glorious mystery, a matter of eternal interest to curious angels (1 Pet. 1:12). Is it any wonder that we must have a world to match the wonder of salvation? Take a look at 2 Peter 3:11–13:

> Since all these things are thus to be dissolved, what sort of people ought you to be in lives of holiness and godliness, waiting for and hastening the coming of the day of God, because of which the heavens will be set on fire and dissolved, and the heavenly bodies will melt as they burn! But according to his promise we are waiting for new heavens and a new earth in which righteousness dwells.

Because we know Jesus is making all things new (Rev. 21:5), and because this passage in 2 Peter 3 itself tells us we are waiting on a new heavens and a new earth, we should not see the fire and dissolution Peter speaks of as annihilating creation but refining it and remaking it. Think of how a blacksmith heats up a piece of metal to soften it before hammering it into shape.

We who trust in Christ are *counted* righteous in Christ—this is our justification—and we are *being made* righteous through the Spirit's sanctifying work in us so that we will be fit to occupy a "sanctified" creation. We are declared God's righteousness (because Christ is our righteousness, 2 Cor. 5:21) so that we will be fit for the land "in which righteousness dwells."

This is the ultimate fruit of gospel mission, and it is undoubtedly what Jesus was praying for when he prayed that God's kingdom would come in such a way that God's will would be done perfectly on earth as it is done in heaven. Jesus himself was the answer to this prayer, inaugurating the kingdom through his earthly ministry and testifying that people who place their faith in him alone will enjoy the blessing of the kingdom's future consummation, when all the crooked ways are finally made straight.

Resurrection Bodies

What will life in the consummated kingdom be like? When God restores what was broken by the fall by delivering a new heavens and a new earth, what will be the role of believers in Christ? Will we be doing that harp-playing thing? There are many possibilities for conjecture; however, we can reasonably ascertain from the Scriptures that those deemed the children of God will assuredly come to reign and rule with God in this new creation in resurrected bodies.

The remaking of creation is not really the highlight of the consummation of redemption. We are. Just as God created Adam to reflect his glory in taking dominion over the created order, in Christ, the new Adam, God is remaking his children to take dominion over the restored creation. Not only is creation made new, but the Bible is pretty clear that you and I are made new and given new bodies. Romans 8:23 says that we are awaiting the redemption of our bodies.

Most days my children don't know that their bodies need redemption. Unless they get sick or fall down, they aren't aware that they are growing up only to have all their strength and vitality removed from them. We learn that as we get older. In fact, the entire point of the last chapter of Ecclesiastes is that our bodies wear out. It doesn't matter how strong our spirit is; Ecclesiastes 12 says that there will come a day where we are tired of being alive. And you've got to remember that death is a part of the fall, and all of us are headed in its direction. It doesn't matter how much spinach we eat, how many pilates classes we take, or how wise we are with life choices—we are going to die and our bodies are going to give out. In fact, I once heard Ray Ortlund say that we spend about a third of our lives asleep in bed recouping our strength, and then we die, which clearly tells us that only Christ is strong.

Christians are to understand that our bodies wear out because we're waiting for the body that doesn't wear out. This new body is not some sort of spiritual, ethereal one. We are awaiting a new physical body. (I know some of you right now are thinking, "Yeah, we're going to need that body so we can play the harp and sing for eternity," which means you're still not getting it.) Check out the epic vision of the tangible new body that Paul gives us in 1 Corinthians 15:35–45:

> But someone will ask, "How are the dead raised? With what kind of body do they come?" You foolish person! What you sow does not come to life unless it dies. And what you sow is not the body that is to be, but a bare kernel, perhaps of wheat or of some other grain. But God gives it a body as he has chosen, and to each kind of seed its own body. For not all flesh is the same, but there is one kind for humans, another for animals, another for birds, and another for fish. There are heavenly bodies and earthly bodies, but the glory of the heavenly is of one kind, and the glory of the earthly is of another. There is one glory of the sun, and another glory of the moon, and another glory of the stars; for star differs from star in glory. So is it with the resurrection of the dead. What is sown is perishable; what is raised is imperishable. It is sown in dishonor; it is raised in glory. It is sown in weakness; it is raised

in power. It is sown a natural body; it is raised a spiritual body. If there is a natural body, there is also a spiritual body. Thus it is written, "The first man Adam became a living being"; the last Adam became a life-giving spirit.

What we see in verses 35–45 is that, no matter how impressive we can make our bodies through a healthy diet, the right exercise, plenty of sleep, good stress management techniques, and books of self-help tips, our body is just a seed. It's not the tree or the flower; it's just the seed. Regardless of how powerful you can make your body, that powerful body is fleeting.

I learned this difficult truth in my cancer diagnosis, simply because, when I had my seizure, I was probably in the best shape of my life, eating the best I had ever eaten, and as strong as I had ever been. In a literal moment it was taken from me. So the Bible teaches that the body you're in—and the eyes that are reading this book—is waning. It is a seed that must die and be replaced.

In 1 Corinthians 15:47–49 Paul compares and contrasts the man of dust (Adam) and the man of heaven (Jesus Christ). All of us, being born of a woman, are born in the image of our first father, Adam. So every one of us has preferred creation to the Creator, every one of us has believed that we're smarter than God, and every one of us has failed to acknowledge him. If Christ tarries, every one of us will die the death of Adam.

Remember that there was no death until sin was introduced into the cosmos. When that fall occurred, death began to reign. You and I are going to physically die, and even if Christ returns before we physically die, we're still going to need a replacement of this perishable body. We will need to put on the imperishable, which is purchased for us by the man of heaven. We will receive new bodies like Christ's resurrection body, and where we once lived as broken images of God, we will at that time bear the image of Jesus who is the perfect image of the invisible God. The brokenness present in each of us will be mended forever, and our eternal, princely bodies will replace our aging flesh. We won't get sick, we won't get hurt, and we won't grow tired. For years I have loved this quote from Augustine's *The City of God*:

> How great shall be that felicity [in the City of God], which shall be tainted with no evil, which shall lack no good, and which shall afford leisure for the praises of God, who shall be all in all! . . . All the members and organs of the incorruptible body, which now we see to be suited to various necessary uses, shall contribute to the praises of God. . . . What power of movement such bodies shall possess, I have not the audacity rashly to define, as I have not the ability to conceive. Nevertheless I will say that in any case, both in motion and at rest, they shall be, as in their appearance, seemly; for into that state nothing which is unseemly shall be admitted God Himself, who is the Author of virtue, shall there be its reward; for, as there is nothing greater or better, He has promised Himself . . . He shall be the end of our desires who shall be seen without end, loved without cloy, praised without weariness. This outgoing of affection, this employment, shall certainly be, like eternal life itself, common to all.[4]

In the new heavens and the new earth, magnifying God without tiring of it will be the duty, the delight, and the activity of all, shared by all who share the life of eternity. Augustine basically says, "Listen, all the energy, all the vitality, that your physical body spends in making itself function will be no more. Your liver won't need to clean your blood. Your kidneys won't have a cleansing function. You won't need those things anymore. All the energy that went into that now goes into praising, ruling, and reigning with God."

Paul knocks it out of the stratosphere in 1 Corinthians 15:54–57:

> When the perishable puts on the imperishable, and the mortal puts on immortality, then shall come to pass the saying that is written:
>
> > "Death is swallowed up in victory."
> > "O death, where is your victory?
> >   O death, where is your sting?"

The sting of death is sin, and the power of sin is the law. But thanks be to God, who gives us the victory through our Lord Jesus Christ.

I have heard this text used shoddily at funerals. Preachers shout, "Where is your sting, O death?" just inches away from an occupied casket. I always want to shout back, "It's right there! There's the sting!"

Do you see in 1 Corinthians 15 when death loses its sting? Do you see when it's swallowed up in victory and can no longer create mourning? It is when we put on the imperishable. So, at funerals we mourn and we hurt; death stings, and there is real loss. This text rightly used at a funeral should point us to the hope of the day where it won't sting any longer.

In that day, the victory of Christ over death will be tangible, palpable, and visceral. We will be given new bodies that are powered by the Spirit and capable of feats unimaginable by our present dimly lit minds. We will be made fit to swim in God's earth-covering glory. It is likely that our resurrected bodies will be like Jesus's resurrected body. His glorified body is perhaps a foreshadow of ours. If he justifies us, he will glorify us (Rom. 8:30).

Living as New Creations

In light of this epic vision of the consummation of the kingdom, Paul charges us: "Therefore, my beloved brothers, be steadfast, immovable, always abounding in the work of the Lord, knowing that in the Lord your labor is not in vain" (1 Cor. 15:58).

Because we understand that this life is perishable and these bodies are seeds, we live and see the world differently. We're much more willing to serve, much more willing to sacrifice, and much more willing to endure discomfort because we know that this broken life is momentary. We see this sentiment in Paul's writing all the time, as he describes current suffering as "light momentary affliction" (2 Cor. 4:17), and then he goes on to list things that are far beyond light but are nevertheless momentary. When we see life in the here and now as momentary and our physical bodies as seeds that must go in the ground to die as a precursor to being raised with the risen Christ, a boldness for Jesus results that is absent when we see our lives in terms of "This life is all there is, so I've got to maximize my pleasure and comfort and joy right now, and I need to experience all the life I can now."

The Bible clearly says that the quickest way to lose your life is to try to save it, and the way to save your life is to lose it (Mark 8:35). First Corinthians 15:58 tells us how to apply that truth to the knowledge of God's restoration of all things in the consummation of history.

As we wind down this chapter, a visiting of the Bible's final scene is in order, and few descriptions of what we see in Revelation's finale are as captivating and poignant as N. T. Wright's. The following is from his book *Surprised by Hope*:

> We thus arrive at . . . perhaps the greatest image of new creation, of cosmic renewal, in the whole Bible. This scene, set out in Revelation 21–22 is not well enough known or pondered (perhaps because, in order to earn the right to read it, one should really read the rest of the Revelation of St John first, which proves too daunting for many). This time the image is that of marriage. The New Jerusalem comes down out of heaven like a bride adorned for her husband.
>
> We notice right away how drastically different this is from all those would-be Christian scenarios in which the end of the world story is the Christian going off to heaven as a soul, naked and unadorned, to meet its maker in fear and trembling. As in Philippians 3, it is not we who go to heaven; it is heaven that comes to earth. Indeed, it is the church itself, the heavenly Jerusalem, that comes down to earth. This is the ultimate rejection of all types of Gnosticism, of every worldview that sees the final goal as the separation of the world from God, of the physical from the spiritual, or earth from heaven. It is the final answer to the Lord's Prayer, that God's kingdom will come and his will be done on earth as in heaven. It is what Paul is talking about in Ephesians 1:10, that God's design, and promise, was to sum up all things in Christ,

things both in heaven and on earth. It is the final fulfillment, in richly symbolic imagery, of the promise of Genesis 1, that the creation of male and female would together reflect God's image into the world. And it is the final accomplishment of God's great design, to defeat and abolish death forever—which can only mean the rescue of creation from its present plight of decay.[5]

Wright then expounds on how the new creation is the fulfillment of God's idea of fruitfulness in the creative order:

Heaven and earth, it seems, are not after all poles apart, needing to be separated forever when all the children of heaven have been rescued from this wicked earth. Nor are they simply different ways of looking at the same thing, as would be implied by some kinds of pantheism. No, they are different, radically different, but they are made for each other in the same way (Revelation is suggesting) as male and female. And when they finally come together, that will be cause for rejoicing in the same way a wedding is: a creational sign that God's project is going forward; that opposite poles within creation are made for union, not competition; that love and not hate have the last word in the universe; that fruitfulness and not sterility is God's will for creation.

What is promised in this passage is what Isaiah foresaw: a new heaven and a new earth, replacing the old heaven and the old earth, which were bound to decay. This doesn't mean . . . that God will wipe the slate clean and start again. If that were so, there would be no celebration, no conquest of death, no long preparation now at last complete. As the chapter develops, the bride, the wife of the Lamb, is described lovingly: she is the new Jerusalem promised by the prophets of the Exile, especially Ezekiel. But, unlike in Ezekiel's vision, where the rebuilt Temple takes eventual center stage, there is no Temple in this city (21:22). The Temple in Jerusalem was always designed, it seems, as a pointer to, and an advance symbol for, the presence of God himself. When the reality is there, the signpost is no longer necessary. As in Romans and 1 Corinthians, the living God will dwell with and among his people, filling the city with his life and love, and pouring out grace and healing in the river of life that flows from the city out to the nations. There is a sign here of the future project that awaits the redeemed in God's eventual new world. So far from sitting on clouds playing harps, as people often imagine, the redeemed people of God in the new world will be the agents of his love going out in new ways, to accomplish new creative tasks, to celebrate and extend the glory of his love.[6]

So you and I will not be like Tom and Jerry playing harps; rather, we will be in a new creation with a new body working unencumbered by the weight of decay, sin, and rebellion for the glory of our great God and king. In worship? Yes. But in worship far more than just song.

This is where we look in hope, this is what we pray toward, and this is what we long for as we grow weary of this broken world. This is why we fast and yearn for his coming. This is why John wraps up the revelation by saying, "Come, Lord Jesus!" (Rev. 22:20). One can practically hear his broken breathlessness.

When we look at the gospel from the air, through the grand narrative of the Scriptures, we see that the gospel is not just about God's forgiving us of sins and giving us eternal life, but also about what we are being forgiven *for* and what eternal life is *like*. We cannot, as some say, deny that God's plan to restore all things is the gospel (as we'll see in chapter 10), because the Scriptures show us that Christ's atoning work is good news for fallen creation. Through the good news of Jesus's life, death, and resurrection, we are reconciled to God in view of our inheritance of the "all things" God is also reconciling (Rom. 8:32). In other words, viewing the gospel from the air shows us its overarching narrative and reveals that it isn't just of first importance (see 1 Cor. 15:3), but of all importance. It is imperative that our gospel take the shape of the Scripture's epic vision of God's redemptive plan. It is imperative that we embrace a gospel that is scaled to the glory of God.

PART THREE

Implications and Applications

9

Dangers in a Gospel on the Ground Too Long

The explicit gospel holds the gospel on the ground and the gospel in the air as complementary, two views of the same redemptive plan God has for the world in the work of his Son. By holding these perspectives together, we do the most justice to the Bible's multifaceted way of proclaiming the good news. When we don't hold them together, either by over-affirming one or dismissing (or outright rejecting) the other, we create an imbalance that leads to all sorts of biblical error.

There are dangers in a gospel that's either on the ground or in the air for too long. But before we survey several dangers in a gospel that stays on the ground too long, we must say a few things about the idea of a slippery slope. A *slippery slope* is simply an idea or action that creates movement in thinking or doing that takes you farther than you originally intended to go or beyond what you first believed. People who prefer the gospel on the ground and criticize the idea of the gospel in the air tend to say something along these lines: "That sort of approach will lead to increasing errors. History shows us that this perspective will lead to the social gospel and other sorts of liberalism."

The first thing we should say in response is that this slippery slope, although seen clearly throughout history, is not sloped at a ninety-degree angle; in other words, this slope is not a cliff. Second, though, because we're all sinful human beings, and every single one of us is prone to overreaction, this slippery slope really affects everyone. There isn't a theology or doctrine out there that it doesn't touch. No one angle has a monopoly on temptation to sliding down into error.

We can see this effect cautioned against in the Scriptures in the tension between grace and works. There are some who ride the pendulum swing all the way into a notion of grace that excludes the necessity of Christian obedience. Paul addresses this clearly in Romans 6:1–2, where he says, "Are we to continue in sin that grace may abound? By no means!" Paul is saying that the grace of a truly regenerate heart will be revealed, as evidence of the Spirit's regenerate effects, by *works*. James agrees (James 2:14–26).

Others ride the pendulum to the other side by overemphasizing works. They take God's clear and good commands and the countless exhortations to obey them and argue that we are somehow partnering with God in our justification. The tension between faith and works, between law and gospel, is always in our hearts, and we see Paul and others speaking to this tension in the Scriptures over and over again.

Another place we see the danger of the slippery slope is in 1 Corinthians 10, where Paul explores the tension between Christian freedom and antinomianism—the idea that we don't need the law anymore, that we are not required to obey the commands of God anymore—and between holiness and legalism. In 1 Corinthians 10:23 he writes, "'All things are lawful,' but not all things are helpful. 'All things are lawful,' but not all things build up." One of the things I've learned as the pastor of a young church is that people who have felt constrained by the law, when we open up the door of liberty, tend to run a million miles an hour through it and end up using their newfound liberty as license. So we have to constantly pull them back to the reality that liberty in Christ and freedom from the law have been given for the good of our brothers and sisters.

We see the slippery slope at work in the early church's battle against heresy. The real problem with the slippery slope is the element of truth in the initial sliding steps down the slope. Would any good Christian deny the reality of grace or the doctrine of *sola gratia*, grace alone? And yet isn't that where the error of easy believism starts? Antinomianism begins with the essential truth of *sola gratia*. So it is not usually in the affirmation of a truth that someone goes down the slippery slope, but in the denial of corresponding truths. In other words, you take what is true beyond its biblical bounds. We see this throughout church history in Arianism, modalism, Pelagianism, adoptionism, Nestorianism, tritheism, universalism, and other heresies. What has happened in each of these errors and others is that someone took an element of what was true and perverted it to the point of heresy, and these are heresies that rear their heads still today.

Even in some of the Reformed circles I run in, among guys who love their Bibles and are zealous for good doctrine, I encounter biblical errors, because it is dangerously easy to take one truth to the exclusion of the whole of what God has revealed. So, for instance, we sometimes see, in relation to the biblical doctrine of God's sovereignty, a lack of missions or prayer, or making God the cause of evil. Some may take the true doctrine of total depravity and slide down the slope into teaching a lack of human responsibility or a downplaying of human value. The bottom line is that it really doesn't matter what doctrine we look at. When sinful men are involved, the slippery slope is always possible.

The good news is that the Scriptures and the testimony of history show us what these slopes are, how the slopes operate, and what trajectories they take. We can't let historical mistakes define our ministries. We have to let the Scriptures do that. But we can see from those mistakes where the land mines and traps are so that we might be faithful to the Scriptures without repeating the errors of the past.

Therefore, as we look in this chapter and the next at some of the biblical and historical slopes that have occurred in response to the two perspectives—the gospel on the ground and the gospel in the air—it is important to understand that the concerns expressed are not foregone conclusions *but possibilities*. And if we don't give special care to watch out for these historic errors, the possibilities become probabilities. Again, I am not saying that someone stuck on the ground or in the air for too long *will* do these things, but rather that history and the Scriptures show us that these things are possibilities that must be guarded against.

What are some dangers, then, when the gospel stays on the ground too long and isn't balanced with a look at the gospel from the air, as it should?

Danger 1: Missing God's Grand Mission

If we stay focused on the gospel on the ground, the first possibility that can become a probability, if not guarded against, is losing our understanding of God's missional plan for every area of life. One of the things I constantly want to teach the people of The Village is a view of God's sovereignty that makes sense to every area of life. One of my favorite texts reflecting this idea is Psalm 139. Somehow Psalm 139 got hijacked by women's ministries, and although I think it's important for women to understand they are fearfully and wonderfully made and not get into the silly game of comparing themselves to everyone around them, I think this text is far weightier than that.

> For you formed my inward parts;
>> you knitted me together in my mother's womb.
> I praise you, for I am fearfully and wonderfully made.
> Wonderful are your works;
>> my soul knows it very well.
> My frame was not hidden from you,
> when I was being made in secret,
>> intricately woven in the depths of the earth.
> Your eyes saw my unformed substance;
> in your book were written, every one of them,
>> the days that were formed for me,
>> when as yet there was none of them. (Ps. 139:13–16)

I love that passage for two reasons. First, it says that God knit me together in my mother's womb. He intricately wove my frame. My external, physical body was created and wired by God in respect to how God knew he was going to use my days. I have always had what adults call "a voice that carries." In fact, one of the great ironies of my life is that what I now get paid to do, I used to get detention for. I don't possess the ability to whisper. By my design, by my genetic makeup, I am loud. I can't lean over and whisper in such a way that other people in the room can't hear me. I simply don't have that ability. So my physical frame—6 feet, 4 inches, 200 pounds, and gangly—was wired by God, designed by him in my mother's womb. This gives me nothing to boast about physically, but it tells me that before I was conceived, God had a plan for my physical makeup that was in keeping with his mission.

Second, not only has God been involved in wiring my physical, external self, but he has also been involved in wiring my internal and emotional self. While verse 13 says, "For you formed my inward parts; you knitted me together in my mother's womb," verse 16 says, "Your eyes saw my unformed substance." Verse 16 tells me that my emotional makeup—the essence of the personality that is naturally in me—was placed in there by God. God wired me physically and emotionally for his good and for his glory throughout the days he had planned for me before one of them was lived out.

Have you noticed that certain people are drawn toward certain hobbies? There is an intrinsic response to certain activities: "Oh, I like that," or, "That's boring." I have a good friend whose dad loves baseball. While he was growing up, his dad took him to baseball games and wanted to play catch with him out in the backyard. That dad loved baseball, but my friend hates it to this day. He has a great relationship with his dad, but the baseball thing never really stuck. He just wasn't a fan of baseball. He is drawn much more to other things.

There is an intrinsic clicking in our soul that draws us toward the things that we're drawn to. I think Psalm 139 is revealing that that clicking is God-ordained, that that is God's *stuff*, that God is doing this in us for his purposes. Notice how Paul addresses this notion in his sermon from Acts 17:

> The God who made the world and everything in it, being Lord of heaven and earth, does not live in temples made by man, nor is he served by human hands, as though he needed anything, since he himself gives to all mankind life and breath and everything. And he made from one man every nation of mankind to live on all the face of the earth, having determined allotted periods and the boundaries of their dwelling place, that they should seek God, in the hope that they might feel their way toward him and find him. Yet he is actually not far from each one of us, for "In him we live and move and have our being." (vv. 24–28)

Acts 17 takes the idea that I have been uniquely wired by God and moves it to the idea that I've been uniquely *placed* by God. The boundaries of my habitation and the allotted times of my life, according to Acts 17, were set for me according to the pre-determined plan of God. I am uniquely wired, and I am uniquely placed. Verse 27 connects this to the hope that men might feel their way toward God and find him because "he is actually not far from each one of us." We may lose the expansiveness of what God means to do in our personal relationship with him if our gospel focus is only on that personal relationship.

It is my understanding from the Scriptures that I live in the neighborhood I live in according to the predetermined plan of God, and I have been uniquely wired and drawn toward certain things so that men might know God, hear from God, see the gospel, hear the gospel, gravitate toward the gospel, and have it preached and proclaimed to them. So when I go to my house after I'm done at the office, it is my understanding that I am not in that neighborhood by mistake. My neighbors on the left, on the right, and directly across the street, are there by the design of God in order that his gospel might be heralded by me to them. I want to see the gym that way; I want to see the coffee shop that way; I want to see the parents in the bleachers with me watching my son's flag football games that way; I want to see my daughter's dance recitals that way. I want to see the entire world through the lens of how God has wired me and where he has placed me for his glory.

We can miss this greater context of God's mission if we only see the gospel as personal. That's just one erroneous step toward seeing the gospel as *private*.

Danger 2: A Rationalized Faith

The slope gets slipperier. Once we give in to the idea that the gospel is only about a personal relationship with God and not about God's redemptive plan to renew all things, we give ourselves permission to stop engaging the world around us. Once we are no longer engaging the world around us with the gospel of Jesus Christ, once we're no longer caring for the widow and the orphan in their distress but allowing someone else to do it, then we've removed one of the major components of true biblical discipleship.

One of the ways the mission of God to reconcile all things to himself chisels away at us in the work of sanctification is when we engage with the hurt, the pain, and the sorrow of the world around us. When we do that, God shows us our inadequacies, shortcomings, and fears. We are shown the places where we don't trust God with our money or our talents. Engaging the city around us and ministering to its needs reveal to us the remaining bastions of sin in our lives, the areas we refuse to surrender to God. In the end, if we stay too long with the gospel on the ground, discipleship can become about a mere transfer of information that doesn't produce maturity or foster internal growth in the fruit of the Spirit.

When discipleship is no longer about a way of living but about information to be learned, a compartmentalization takes place in our spiritual thinking that results in hypocrisy. We can end up with a church that does not see confession and repentance as ongoing ethics but rather simply as truths that need to be defended. So instead of being missional in our understanding of the world, we become defensive in posture. Instead of following Jesus, we circle the wagons.

I'm well aware that there are things that need to be guarded against out there; we are commanded to contend for the faith and watch our doctrine closely (Jude 3; 1 Tim. 4:16). But as I outlined in chapter 7, on reconciliation, the primary Christian posture is not defensive but offensive. We are called not to set up shop and ward others off but to be on mission with God. We contend for the faith and guard sound doctrine *while we are on mission* as a component of mission.

When I first began pastoring The Village Church, the first thing I did was preach through the book of Ephesians. I did so because The Village had begun to die. When I started, the church was called Highland Village First Baptist Church, and it had shrunk down to about one hundred members, had a bit of debt, was very confused theologically and missiologically, and was just in a general state of messiness. I decided to preach through Ephesians, because one of the things that we get a good picture of in Ephesians is the birth and death of a church.

In Acts 19 we see the founding of the church at Ephesus, and it's pretty spectacular. Apollos goes in and does some teaching about Jesus. The Bible doesn't really let us know what he left out, but Priscilla and Aquila have to pull him aside and explain to him more fully the way of God. Then Apollos leaves, and Paul comes to town, bringing the Holy Spirit with him. The church takes off. Paul is doing miracles and preaching the kingdom, and amazing things are happening. In fact, he goes daily to the hall of Tyrannus, and we are told, "This continued for two years, so that all the residents of Asia heard the word of the Lord, both Jews and Greeks" (v. 10). How incredible is that? (Paul's mission in Ephesus is so effective and undeniable that even the demonic forces in that area had heard of him.) In verses 21–41, we see that the gospel has taken root in such a way that the whole socioeconomic climate of Ephesus begins to change. Those who had made money off of sinful things were no longer able to make money off those things, simply because of the pervasiveness of the gospel in the culture.

The transformation in Ephesus is extraordinary and powerful. In Acts 20, then, Paul is on his way to Jerusalem, knowing he's going to be arrested, knowing that it's probably the beginning of the end for his ministry, and he gathers the Ephesian elders and basically tells them, "I am clean when it comes to you. I'm clean, because I have proclaimed the whole council of God to you." And then, inspired by the Holy Spirit, he tells them that, when he leaves, wolves are going to come in and devour the sheep, that false teachers will rise up within the church, and that some of those very elders will be in that group that leads people astray into perversions of the truth. Then Paul prays over the Ephesian elders, and he is gone.

The book of Ephesians is Paul's letter to the Christians at Ephesus, which he writes from prison in Rome. In this letter, he admonishes the church at Ephesus to speak the truth, to put away falsehood. The main themes of his letter are Christ reconciling all creation to himself, Christ uniting people from all the nations to himself, and Christ joining people to one another in his church. Although these emphases hint at the projected needs of the Ephesian church, we don't learn a great deal from this epistle as to what was happening in the church in Ephesus from a doctrinal standpoint.

But in 1 and 2 Timothy, Paul is writing to Timothy, who is an elder in Ephesus, and it's interesting to note that within a decade of Paul's prophecy in Acts 20 that wolves would attack and false teachers would arise, his prediction has come true. Paul then coaches Timothy through the Ephesian controversy and commands him to fight heresy and instruct the church extensively in the role of the gospel. Paul is teaching his son in the faith, Timothy, to use the gospel to combat the Ephesian controversy, which had to do with some who were attempting to change the nature of the gospel.

Implications and Applications

Then we come to 1 and 2 John. John is an elder in Ephesus. (On a side note, it has always blown my mind that there was this level of pastoral skill at Ephesus, yet even with this A-team of pastoral care, the church was slipping into false teaching.) In his letters, John appeals for love and grace but also for the combating of those who feel they have no need to confess or repent of sin.

These are glimpses into the stages of the church at Ephesus. In Revelation 2, however, we see what's going to be the death of that church:

> To the angel of the church in Ephesus write: "The words of him who holds the seven stars in his right hand, who walks among the seven golden lampstands. I know your works, your toil and your patient endurance, and how you cannot bear with those who are evil, but have tested those who call themselves apostles and are not, and found them to be false. I know you are enduring patiently and bearing up for my name's sake, and you have not grown weary. But I have this against you, that you have abandoned the love you had at first. Remember therefore from where you have fallen; repent, and do the works you did at first. If not, I will come to you and remove your lampstand from its place, unless you repent." (vv. 1–5)

What's clear is that, even in this late stage of the game, the Ephesians are doing some things very well. In verse 2, we see that they have patient endurance, they cannot bear with those who are evil, and they have tested false apostles. They know doctrine well enough to know true teaching from false. They are patiently enduring the suffering they are experiencing. We can sum all of those characteristics into two things: enduring pain and contending for sound doctrine. On paper, this sounds like a church I want to be a part of. This sounds like a church I want to send my kids to and see them grow into the fullness of Christ. But there is that word of warning too: "But I have this against you, that you have abandoned the love you had at first. Remember therefore from where you have fallen; repent, and do the works you did at first."

They've abandoned their first love. We often hear this as a kind of ethereal, elevated, sentimentalized love for Jesus. But I think we can dig deeper than that. I think the key to this text is to look at what he tells them to do. "Remember therefore from where you have fallen; repent, and do the works you did at first." Then the threat is this: "If you don't repent, your lampstand is going to be removed and the church is going to cease to be" (v. 5).

Here's the big question: What were they doing at first that was so important to get back to doing? If we return to their beginning in Acts 19 and look at what marked them as a congregation, we see this:

> Also many of those who were now believers came, confessing and divulging their practices. And a number of those who had practiced magic arts brought their books together and burned them in the sight of all. And they counted the value of them and found it came to fifty thousand pieces of silver. So the word of the Lord continued to increase and prevail mightily. (vv. 18–20)

One of the things we see happening early on at Ephesus is a raw, gritty admission of shortcoming and guilt, but somehow, over time, Ephesus had become civilized and somewhat cold and obsessively acute in their doctrinal awareness, so they aligned themselves with what was true but lost their missional edge. They had embraced an overly rationalized faith. Their head was in the right place, but their heart had not followed. They had the appearance of godliness but denied the power therein to produce radical affection for Jesus, radical repentance from sin, and radical love for a lost world. In the end, they were so proud and so far from the Lord that Jesus had to say, "I'm going to remove my light from you if you don't get back to doing what you did at first."

It is highly likely that the church at Ephesus had gone down the slippery slope from doctrinal precision to doctrinal arrogance, transferring its affections for Christ and its neighbors to intellectualism, and suddenly the Ephesian believers were no longer dealing with witches, sorcerers, and sexual deviance, no longer grappling with their own sin, and no longer making the gospel primary in regard to its reconciling work among them and around the world. They had grown civilized, and their faith had grown rationalized. This happens to any of us if we stop seeing the bigger picture of the gospel and go into hyper-focus on the micro-image of "my faith." Our intellect comes to fill the temple of our hearts, and we no longer tremble in fear and give ourselves to a mind-set of mission in response to the manifest glory of God, like Isaiah did, because we've simply stopped seeing it. Our view is on the ground so long that we've cropped the fullness of God's majesty from the frame.

Danger 3: A Self-Centered Gospel

These errors lead us down the slippery slope to what I think is the last and most significant danger of a gospel on the ground too long. When we over-emphasize the perspective of the gospel on the ground, we make the gospel increasingly individualistic. We make the gospel man-centered. We make it *self*-centered.

No one plays this game better than the Pharisees and the scribes. Let's look at Luke 15, beginning in verse 1: "Now the tax collectors and sinners were all drawing near to hear him. And the Pharisees and the scribes grumbled, saying, 'This man receives sinners and eats with them.'" That verse doesn't carry a lot of weight for us because, without some understanding of what's going on historically, we have a tendency to just say, "Oh yeah, well, you're a sinner, I'm a sinner, we're all sinners." And most of us have heard that tax collectors were simply guys who took more money than they should have and pocketed the extra, and that's why everyone hated them. This is not the whole story.

In Jesus's day, Rome ruled the world from India to England, but how did someone govern from India to England in pre-modern times? Let's say that, here in Texas, some of us thought that Texas should be its own country. Let's say we've been out in the woods playing with our Winchesters, and we decide we're seceding from the Union. So there is a rebellion. "We're not taking this stuff anymore, and no one is going to tell us we can't carry our fully automatic rifles into the Tex-Mex restaurant with us!" And we rebel. The United States of America will simply send in a couple of helicopters from the nearest Air Force base and launch a missile from some top-secret bunker, and this thing will be over in minutes.

But that's not how the first-century world worked. So, how did one govern from India to England in the first century without the capabilities of long-range weapons, airplanes, and fast-moving vehicles? The only way was with a massive army, and the only way to provide for and train a massive army was through taxes. So the tax collectors were hated by the Jews simply because they raised money for an occupying pagan force that was oppressive and had likely killed or hurt someone they knew. Tax collectors were a despised class, and yet they were drawn toward the gospel.

There were also "sinners" present. Although we know we're sinners and that everyone is a sinner, sinners in the first century were a class of people. They had disreputable jobs or pasts, or they had some sort of disease or malformation that caused people to say, "God has judged them." Sinners weren't allowed in worship services; they were pushed out to the margins of community life, which is why the Samaritan woman at the well came to draw water in the heat of the day instead of the cool of the morning.

Here's the scene: tax collectors and sinners are drawing near to hear the gospel from the center of the gospel himself, Jesus. But they're not the only ones there: "And the Pharisees and the scribes grumbled, saying, 'This man receives sinners and eats with them.'"

One of the things that happens when we no longer buy into God's being for the least of these, when we don't hear him calling *us* to engage the world around us in its pain and injustice, is the stalling out of discipleship. Our faith simply becomes about us and the Lord and getting our ticket to heaven. There is a kernel of truth in the notion that "Jesus would have died for you if you were the only one who ever lived," but the truth is you aren't the only one who ever lived. Moreover, dismissing the gospel in the air to hyper-focus on the gospel on the ground easily tempts us to begin to think of the gospel as all about us, not God. When we zoom out and look at the Scripture's overarching story line, viewing the gospel in the air, we see that God's story of redemption has Christ at the center and his glory as its chief concern. Missing this makes the gospel man-centered.

Once again, this perverts our relationship with the Lord and our calling to be agents of reconciliation in the world around us. When we stay focused on the ground too long, we can make the faith individualistic instead of reconciling and missional.

If we stay focused on the ground too long, we begin to read the Bible with ourselves at the center. This is just a short slide away from the worst forms of sectarianism and isolationism. This is a great way to become prideful and arrogant, to rationalize disobedience to the Great Commission and the Great Commandment. It is a great way to give up on mission or evangelism. In a weird sort of irony, both hyper-Arminian revivalism and hyper-Calvinistic insulation have at their root a self-centered gospel.

But there are dangers in staying in the air too long, as well.

10

Dangers in a Gospel in the Air Too Long

Something subtle but dangerous happens when the gospel is put purely in terms of God's restoration of all things: it becomes easy to embrace the biblically deficient "social gospel." A cosmic view of the gospel enables us to see that God's plan of redemption encompasses all of creation. It includes a reversal of the curse of the fall in all its ramifications, but it is centralized in God's love for sinful man, Christ's sacrifice for man's justification, and Christ's resurrection for man's eternal life. The social gospel, however, isn't just something God does; man plays a vital role too. Red flags should go up, for instance, when we see the phrase "Be the gospel" or hear the unfortunately oft-repeated line, "Preach the gospel at all times; if necessary, use words."[1]

The danger in holding the gospel in the air too long is skittering out to the slippery slope of the social gospel. When we obscure or lose the primary and central truth that is revealed as we view the gospel on the ground, it becomes difficult to distinguish the function of the gospel from a Buddhist's acts of charity or an atheist's act of altruism.

Danger 1: Syncretism

If the danger of focusing too long on the gospel on the ground is essentially *sectarianism*, the danger of focusing too long on the gospel in the air is definitely *syncretism*. In other words, if being on the ground too long leads us to withdraw from the world and disengage from mission, then being in the air too long almost always leads the church to look indistinguishable from the world.

Syncretism starts innocently enough. It never starts with a plan to subvert or crush the true gospel. In fact, what I have found, in my look into church history and in meeting with certain pastors, is that those who fall into syncretism almost always started out with a pure motive to see people know, love, and follow Jesus. They fall off track, however, if they become dominated by frustration at others' failures or at the state of the world. Many of those who end up living just like the world but still want to call themselves Christians point toward the failures of the past generation to feed the poor, take care of the homeless, battle for racial equality, and the like. They'll point toward the established church's buildings, programs, and major emphases as evidence for what they see as omissions from the full gospel.

Many of their frustrations are valid; they are usually on to something. But as this youthful angst plays out, as they see the commands of God to love the hurting and broken driving them to do just that, they run into the hardness of some Christians, which drives them into using guilt as a motivating force for action. Once guilt is the motivating factor instead of the gospel itself, we've got a salvation based on works instead of on grace. So instead of God's love being the driving force of our engagement with those who need to hear about that love, we do those things because we've been led to feel guilty about not doing them. Suddenly, mission is works-driven, not gospel-driven. That's the first syncretistic step, because it conflates Christian mission with works religion, which is a false gospel, and it happens to be the root of every religion that *isn't* Christian.

We see the veneer of syncretism, if not much more of it, every time we see Christians emphasizing "making the world a better place" over the salvation of the world from personal sin by a personal Savior sent by a personal God. In some of these Christian campaigns, it is difficult to find anything distinctly Christian about the message. The gospel has been subsumed by a message any religious person (or irreligious person) with a mind to help their fellow man could get behind. That is part of the design in the syncretistic impulse—attract people to the gospel by highlighting the way the gospel speaks to economic justice, for instance, or saving the Brazilian rainforest—but almost invariably these emphases become missions of a different sort. The Bible does not teach justification by recycling, but it would be hard to tell that from some Christian organizations that have been in the air so long that their feet no longer touch the ground.

The mission becomes vague when it stays zoomed out. We lose belief and don't miss it, because we've traded it in for social action. What happens in full-blown syncretism is the merging of biblical truth with idolatry. People don't choose idolatry because it doesn't look appealing. Yet in the worst forms of syncretistic Christian mission, ample room is given to pluralistic approaches to faith, new-age sentimentalism, and heresies that sell more books than the unadulterated gospel. Jesus ends up becoming a figure on a shelf of gods we've sinfully labeled "Christian."

Danger 2: A Christless Gospel

Once that first level of syncretism takes place, and we're out there doing the things that the Bible commands us to do in confronting systemic levels of injustice, sorrow, and poverty, and seeking gospel interactions with worldly people and powers, one of the things we learn very quickly is that people are offended by the message of Christ's atoning work on the cross. Christ's death on the cross is an indictment of how horrific we are at our core, and nothing is more frustrating to those outside of our faith than to come to the realization that they are broken and sinful by nature—not just by their actions but *by their nature*. Most people today find it easy to compare themselves to their neighbors, or to somebody they know who "really has issues," or maybe even to the criminal they see on the news, and feel that they are good people. And to think of a God who would kill his own Son in order to save them? They can't fathom it. It doesn't penetrate their hearts and minds. If you remember from our discussion in chapter 4, the gospel message can actually end up hardening its hearers against it.

When people stay in the air too long, they can begin to try to make the gospel more palatable, because they desperately want people to know and love Jesus. As they are feeding the poor, building homes for those without homes, and engaging in these systemic parts of the suffering of our world, they begin to water down the gospel message. They take the clear commands of Scripture and begin to tweak them in the hopes that some might believe and be saved. In essence, they try to save the gospel by changing the gospel.

Based on what I've seen in my travels, I cannot note this strongly enough. It is important that pastors and all believers in Jesus Christ know and understand that we will never make the gospel so attractive that everyone wants to submit to it. According to the Scriptures, the message will be the stench of death to those who are perishing (2 Cor. 2:16). So it doesn't matter how you dress, what technology you use in your services, or what creative props you've got on your stage—if you're preaching the biblical gospel, there will be those who want nothing to do with it. A lot of what I see and read in books that specifically target young evangelicals reflects the idea that if we would simply create a comfortable experience and not harp on secondary issues, somehow more people will trust in and follow Jesus Christ. So we lop off large swaths of the Bible because it won't appeal to our target demographic.

If we will just look at history, seeing the philosophy and work of Walter Rauschenbusch and the Social Gospel Movement that occurred in the late 1800s, what we'll see happening is the stunning disappearance of the atoning work of Jesus Christ on the cross over a period of time. Historically, the way it works is that little concessions are made on what people would call "secondary issues." The idea is to compromise on some things and hope to meet in the middle at the central thing. But those who hate the true gospel and love themselves always insist that the atoning work of Christ is a secondary issue. This is how the doctrine of penal substitution has come to be considered a secondary issue and why many have wanted to pull it off the table altogether. So when guys who emphasize the gospel on the ground get nervous about terms such as *missional* and cautious about the idea of a church being for the city, it's usually with good reason, because history shows us where this trajectory often goes.

Really, the issue is not with the meta-narrative or social justice but with those who stay in the air too long and leave the atoning work of Christ behind as they press into God's call to care for the poor, the widow, and the orphan, engaging in works of justice and mercy in only vaguely biblical or theistic ways. People are absolutely right about this fear only to the extent that the gospel in the air obscures the atoning work of Christ, or the point at which doing so makes the true gospel look synonymous with the social gospel of cultural transformation. We would be wrong to say that creation, fall, redemption, and consummation can never be the biblical gospel. (Colossians 1:20 would be Exhibit A in our case.)

Danger 3: Culture as Idol

It's not just historical cautionary tales that cause some anxiety about the missional push. There are plenty of causes for concern in present movements. The drift into Christlessness happens to this day. When we stay in the air too long, we can mistake a sketchy "redemption of all things" for the whole story. The reality is that we can create a utopian idea in our minds of God's cosmic purposes that bears little or no resemblance to how the Bible actually says the gospel affects cultures and systems. The slippery slope from this perspective is to fudge on biblical concepts and promote other ideas that better fit our modern notions of what a redeemed culture looks like.

Implications and Applications

Just consider the slide on this slope within mainline Protestantism in the West when it comes to the issue of women in church leadership. The issue has been viewed basically the same way for two thousand years of church history, a view that can summarize this way: *Men and women have been created equal and yet distinct by God. Men are charged with leading in the home and the church, and women have been given to men as helpmates.* However, as the church began to engage a modern culture, we began to hear questions such as, "Aren't women just as gifted as men? Surely those texts in the Bible can't mean what they appear to say, because, I mean, look at our culture." The frame of reference shifts. The culture begins to define the Scriptures instead of the Scriptures defining the culture.

The egalitarianism in mainline Protestantism is a concession to our culture, a way of rejecting biblical values and saying, "The Bible, when all is said and done, is not our authority. The culture is our authority."

I know this is an offensive charge. I know some will say, "That's not true. I don't think the Scriptures teach what you say they teach. Isn't that just your interpretation of Scripture?" What happens then is a game of textual tennis in which some verses are taken out of context to combat other verses that clearly state how God designed things to work. A chronological snobbery kicks in, where former days are cast as dark and wicked and our current day is the enlightened state of things. Or some point to the abuses of sinful, foolish men and say, "See? That's what happens when you listen to the Scriptures as they are written. Surely that was for their time and does not hold weight in our time."

We tweak verses and say that we stand under the authority of Scripture, but we end up with conclusions that are different from how Scripture has been interpreted or defined for the last two thousand years. What has happened? God's entire design has been deemed outdated or unequipped for the needs of our day.

Culture rather than God now dictates mission, and this is how culture becomes an idol.

We should point out here that Paul never uses a cultural argument in declaring God's design for gender roles; rather, he always points back to God's creative work. Paul shows us how God's design can be *applied* to cultural environs, but he doesn't establish the distinct genders and their distinct roles by the cultural environs. (This is why we say that it is still God's will for women to embrace modesty but not his will that they mustn't braid their hair. The root distinction is eternal; the application is cultural.) If we trusted God, we would believe that he created the world to work in such a way that it leads to our greatest possible joy.

So Paul doesn't argue culture. He doesn't think the role of women in the church is a cultural issue. He doesn't think the problem is the result of some kind of patriarchal brokenness, a rigid system that, in the end, needs to be adhered to in order for men to hold on to power. In fact, it's just the opposite. He will hammer men over and over again for their failure to act as servant leaders who love their wives well. But if we listen to mainline Protestantism on this issue, they would have us know that culture must be our guide.

You may say, "Isn't this a secondary issue, Matt? Why are you starting a fight on this? Can't we disagree here and still partner in gospel ministry?" Sure we can. But my point remains: our trust in Scripture gets rattled and we start to become our own authority—or worse, we let culture dictate to us what's true—and in the end, we begin to slide away from what is clear in Scripture and justify how we read the Scriptures in order to say what we want it to say and make it more palatable to the world around us.

I live in Dallas, Texas, by the design of God Almighty. Churches here are huge. There are multi-thousand-seat auditoriums all over the place. Some of them are filled to the brim week in and week out for multiple services. Texas churches are not secularized as are churches in the Northeast or the Northwest. There are a lot of crosses here. You will see a lot of fish on people's cars. But if you look at Dallas statistically and compare it to more secularized cities, you'll see that we have just as much divorce, adultery, and debt as the world around us. The only place we win is in church attendance. Doesn't this mean we are just as syncretistic as the average Joe in Manhattan or Seattle? We are, and maybe more so. We simply go to church on Sundays because it's more a cultural act than a relational act with the God of the universe.

In this vein, if you move away from the issue of women and move to that of homosexuality, we see the exact same thing happening. In order to be more palatable to the world around us, in order to see more people come to know Jesus Christ, the issue of homosexuality is pushed as a nonissue. "Why can't they do what they want to do? What business is it of ours? Aren't we oppressing people if we tell them what they want to do in the privacy of their own homes is wrong? Surely the Bible is some outdated, worn out old book that has no bearing on today. Who are we to even say that something is wrong?" And on and on we could go. It's the same arguments all over again. I'm not saying that if you're an egalitarian, the next step you will logically take is to affirm homosexuality as a legitimate way of life, but I *am* saying that this is exactly what happened in mainline Protestantism.

Consider the current debates on the existence of hell. Rob Bell jump-started a social media meltdown among evangelicals a while ago by asking some questions about hell and who goes there.[2] Much legitimate debate ensued about how theological discourse should be conducted, but underneath that was a steady stream of wondering, "Isn't hell an outdated doctrine? Do we really need it? Does the Bible really teach it? Couldn't two thousand years of church tradition be wrong?" Suddenly, what the Bible says about God's love and wrath became not as central as how we feel about those ideas. If our idea of what God's love is like doesn't jibe with the Bible's many references to hell, maybe it's not the Bible's references to hell that need tweaking but our view of God's love.

The mainline Protestant's aversion to the traditional view of eternal conscious torment in hell has spilled into evangelicalism. We don't want to talk about it. We don't want to acknowledge it. In many places, we want to deny it. We want to make God into some kind of benevolent fairy who loves everyone in ways that make all the biblical texts on wrath and judgment deniable.

When we stay in the air too long, we lose the gospel center and are in danger of sliding down the slippery slope into a view of cosmic redemption that puts the culture at the center. Whatever we revolve around is what we worship. So, one danger of being in the air too long is idolizing our notion of a redeemed culture, and, of course, the removal of the truth that God is God results in all kinds of other lies.

Danger 4: Abandoning Evangelism

I'm not sure if this is a new phenomenon, but it seems today that many who call themselves Christians have a fundamental aversion to the very idea of conversion or the idea that people need to be converted. We see many people, Christians included, who actually get offended when you talk about reaching people with the gospel. If we say, "We want to see Jews come to know Jesus Christ," a firestorm can result in your city, on the news, or in the paper: "Who are Christians to try to convert Jews? What gives them the right to think Muslims need a new religion? Who are Christians to try to convert Jehovah's Witnesses or Mormons?" The prevailing idea is a caricature of tolerance.

What we're seeing now is the erosion of the mission of God to reconcile all things to himself, which necessarily includes reconciling individuals to himself, by the church's relinquishing of the gospel on the ground. We say, "Let's change our fundamental message in order to see people come to know and love Jesus Christ." This is, of course, nonsensical. It is the gospel that saves.

Despite the fact that the history of syncretism clearly shows us that removing the offensive parts of our faith in order to gain followers merely kills our faith, people continue to try this. As the slide down this slope continues, we see an adherence to substitutionary atonement disappear, because it is by far the most offensive doctrine. Once we remove the bloody atonement as satisfaction of God's wrath for sin, the wheels really come off. Where the substitutionary atoning work of Jesus Christ on the cross is preached and proclaimed, missions will not spin off to a liberal shell of a lifeless message but will stay true to what God has commanded the church to be in the Scriptures.

If you think I am too hard on mainline Protestantism, all you have to do is look at its declining numbers. It has lost the *evangel*, which means it doesn't care about evangelism. Those involved major in social transformation, which can be obtained without church. Additionally, you don't need to come to church and be discipled if there isn't sin to be atoned for and repented of. If there isn't in the end a need to be sanctified by the ongoing work of the Holy Spirit, there certainly isn't a need to be under the authority of a Bible-holding governing body of elders or pastors who can exercise church discipline, watch carefully over your soul, and make sure you are growing in your relationship with God. So what's left of mainline Protestantism is an array of dwindling institutions that do good for people in small ways at the expense of their eternal souls.

To fill empty bellies, to build shelters for the homeless, and to put silver and gold in the cups of beggars without any concern for the eternal nature of their souls is an exercise of futility. Our hope should always be the gospel. Our hope should always be that people would hear, understand, and come to know God in a powerful way. When we become synchronized to the way of the world around us, we cease to be on God's mission. Sharing the gospel on the ground is the sharp edge of gospel mission; if we lose that, we lose real mission. If we lose evangelism, we may as well be the Peace Corps, helping people in the here and now but not giving two cents if they go to hell. Let's not create a mission that makes us feel better about ourselves but doesn't solve anything in regard to the deepest hurts of humanity.

Without a heart transformed by the grace of Christ, we just continue to manage external and internal darkness. It's like mowing over the weeds without removing them. Here in Texas, the weeds will grow before the grass does, and they grow ten times as fast as the grass. So when you mow your lawn, as soon as you're done mowing your lawn, it looks perfect. It all looks like grass: it all looks good and it all looks healthy. But a day or two later, you'll begin to see the weeds that grow so much faster shoot up in your lawn and reveal that a lot of your lawn isn't grass at all but rather weeds. The only way to kill those weeds is not to mow over them but remove them. The only thing that has that kind of effect on the human soul is the gospel of Jesus Christ. When we do acts of mercy and justice without the gospel as our motivation and without the gospel as our hope to share, we're really chasing the wind.

I want to reiterate that these current examples I'm giving are only here to remind us that there are land mines that need to be watched out for and that the failures of others in the past shouldn't stop us from being obedient to God's command to care for the poor and to be a faithful presence in all the domains of our culture. One of the great ironies in modern evangelicalism, and one of the things that is heartbreaking for me as a minister of the gospel of Jesus Christ, is to watch friends align themselves with only one of these perspectives, either the gospel on the ground or the gospel in the air. They argue and blame one another for why more people aren't coming to know the Lord. People who identify more with the ground perspective look at those who are on mission in regard to acts of justice and mercy in their cities and say that they're part of the problem. They may simply hear the phrase "gospel of the kingdom" and immediately think, "Oh, that's emergent. That's liberal." Or they'll hear about being "for the city" and think, "Oh man, it's only a matter of time before you deny the atonement."

Implications and Applications

This might have been true in the past, and it might even be true in some places right now, but the existence of dangers doesn't necessarily mean that those brothers who affirm the importance of viewing the gospel in the air don't love the atoning work of Christ like you do. So it's a great idea to simply get to know those brothers and find out what they do believe and if they do proclaim the atoning work of Christ before we throw grenades at them. My hope is that we will see much more charitable debate and much less friendly fire around these issues.

Likewise, if we talk to the guys who are more aligned with the gospel in the air, we find that they are very quick to accuse guys aligned with the gospel on the ground of not loving the mission of God, of being cold and uncaring about the hurts of the world around them, and of simply wanting to cling to their doctrine in "clanging cymbal" ways (1 Cor. 13:1). Once again, I encourage these critics to get to know people before they cast aspersions. What I have found over and over again is that we sinners love to build straw men to attack or consider one camp's worst example as normative for everyone else who may lean that way. Let's stop being ridiculous. My hope is that we would quit blaming one another and begin faithfully learning from one another how to avoid the land mines that can befall all of us.

Oftentimes it's not spokespeople who are blamed but rather their fans and followers. "It's not really this guy or that guy," some say; "it's their disciples who are really the problem." Although I think there might be some legitimacy to that, I still encourage you to have conversations. There have been guys about whom I have been told, "They are nonmissional. They are not for engaging the culture around them. They said it at this conference. They wrote about it in that book."

Through the providence of God, I've been able to sit across the table and ask some clarifying questions and find out that guys who have been pegged, specifically by the Reformed missional community, as nonmissional simply aren't nonmissional. Our semantics break down. The staunch, historic Reformed guys will point to others and say, "That missional stuff, that kingdom-of-God stuff, is liberalism." They say that without any real understanding and without having had the conversations with the right guys to see that there is a strong passion among the Reformed missional community to champion the atoning work of Jesus Christ, to affirm imputed righteousness, and to see the blood of the cross as the central message of our churches as we engage the city and reach out in acts of justice and mercy.

The reality is that our sin puts danger before us, no matter where we land philosophically or methodologically. No one is immune from going down a slippery slope. But we should not discount truth because of the existence of abuses. If such a leap is warranted, we might as well join Ghandi in rejecting Christian truth because of the hypocrisy of Christians.

11

Moralism and the Cross

One of the first memories I have of church is when my family was living in the Bay Area outside of San Francisco, in Alameda, California. At a vacation Bible school put on by a Baptist church that was trying to reach families with the gospel of Jesus Christ, we did some crafts, had a story time, and played some games, but what I remember most vividly is gathering in their little sanctuary to sing songs. They were children's songs. We sang one song in particular about God hating liars. In reality the Bible does say that God hates liars, so it's not like they had strayed from some sort of biblical mooring. But I remember thinking, even at a very young age, that I was in trouble. I remember singing the song in a cheerful, clappy way and thinking to myself, "Um, *I* lie. I'm in trouble here." I'm sure, just to give them the benefit of the doubt, that they shared the gospel and talked about the love of God, but I don't remember any of that. I simply remember that God hated liars.

That was my first brush with the moralistic, therapeutic deism that we mentioned in the introduction. If you recall, moral, therapeutic deism is the idea that we are able to earn favor with God and justify ourselves before God by virtue of our behavior. At vacation Bible school in a little Baptist church, I met the arch-nemesis of the gospel of Jesus Christ. This simple song about God hating liars created in me what it aimed to: a desire not to lie in order to win the affection of God. I would battle believing this false gospel for years to come without even knowing it.

As I grew older, I tried to be good. I was just never really good at it. The evangelical atmosphere at the time, especially in the youth-ministry culture in which I found myself, was serious about keeping us young people holy. So from music to movies, from where you could go to where you couldn't, from the right language to use to what you could and couldn't drink, the overarching emphasis of what we were taught was "don't be bad; be good."

As my family moved from the Bay Area to Texas, I ended up, by the grace of God, having a high-school locker next to a junior named Jeff Faircloth. Jeff was aggressive about his faith. He had a deep love for the Lord. In fact, he began to share the gospel with me almost immediately, saying, "Hey, I need to tell you about Jesus. When do you want to do that?" He was going to let me decide where we had the conversation, but having the conversation was not up for debate.

I began to ask Jeff questions about religion and the Bible, and Jeff began to take me to youth group with him, and the more I went to church, the more confused I got and the more I thought that this Christian thing really wasn't for me, because it just looked like moralistic deism. (I didn't know it in those terms at the time, of course; I just knew it was about being well-behaved.) I want to give that church the benefit of the doubt also, assuming that maybe my ears were just closed so I couldn't hear the gospel. Maybe my eyes were closed, and I just couldn't see. But the overwhelming message appeared to me to be more along the lines of, "If you listen to Journey, you're going to do meth and kill your parents. So don't listen to Journey. If you like Journey, then you should like this Christian band. Listen to this Christian band instead. And don't see these kinds of movies, because they are going to lead to premarital sex and cursing." I'm sure they presented in some way that Jesus forgives and that Jesus was my righteousness before God, but all I kept hearing was, "Do this, do this, do this. And don't do that other stuff."

Very early on, it became clear to me that I wasn't a good enough spiritual athlete to make the team. It became crystal clear, as I tried to do good, that I just didn't have the legs for it. I would do really well for a couple of weeks and then stumble and fall. I would resolve to myself, "I'm not going to do these things anymore. I'm going to do these good things instead, and by doing these good things and not doing these bad things, God is going to love me, heal me, and welcome me into his family." I got stuck in a really crazy cycle of attending some youth function, getting all teary-eyed, asking God for forgiveness, and swearing to him that I was never going to do those things again, only to do those things again within a week or two.

Eventually I found myself running from God. I ran because if there was shame to begin with, there was double shame at the moment when I said I wasn't going to do it anymore but then did it. I was caught on a burdensome behavioristic treadmill until Christ opened my heart to him and I began in the power of the gospel to love him and pursue him in deeper ways. But my indwelling sin remained. I wrestled for moral ground but found myself losing much more than winning. Although I was growing in my faith at the time, my inability to sustain repentance continued to be a weight around my soul that kept me from worshiping fully or pursuing Christ with all that was in me. I was stuck in shame over constant stumbling, especially concerning issues of morality that were expressed in the church as being larger than others.

I began to notice, as I shared the gospel with others, that when I brought them to church, they would get confused in the same way. I would try to bring them back to the cross, but what they were hearing was that a Christian looked like Ned Flanders: religiously neat hair, Mr. Rogers cardigan, sappily sanctimonious speech, and consumer of exclusively so-called Christian products. But we weren't like Ned Flanders.[1] Our houses didn't look like Ned Flanders's house. Our families didn't look like his. Our behavior didn't look like his. The feeling became great that something big was really *off* in the church.

The Dirty Rose

This feeling came to a head in my first year of college. I attended a small Baptist college in Abilene in west Texas, and upon my arrival there, I had to sign up for a fine arts course. I'll be straight with you: I'm not a fine arts kind of guy, so I really didn't know what to do. I have a high respect for art, but I don't know that I excel at any part of it. What fit into my schedule was one of two classes. One was pottery, which I was somewhat excited about simply because of the biblical imagery in Romans 9, but at that time the movie *Ghost* had just come out, which had a scene with Patrick Swayze and Demi Moore getting down and muddy at the pottery wheel, and there was just something that weirded me out about that.

Instead of pottery, I chose to take a drama class. In my drama class, I met a woman who had lived in that area her entire life and was trying to get her life back on track. She was several years older than me (in her late twenties), already had a child, and was working at a bar. She was not a church person and had no church background. But what she did have was a dry, sarcastic humor that I thought was brilliant. When you're in a drama class that's weird to begin with, and your professor says, "Be a tree. No, be a tree with more motion. No, be an angry tree," and you have to act out these things, having someone around with a sarcastic sense of humor was a bit of fresh air. So Kim and I hit it off. We laughed a lot, and I began to try to share the gospel with her and to teach her about Jesus's love. I prayed a lot and longed to see her come to a saving knowledge of Jesus Christ.

Along with a couple of my friends, I began serving and encouraging her. We invited her to join us at get-togethers, and when she had to go to work sometimes we would watch her daughter for her.

In the middle of all that, a friend of mine was coming to do a concert in a nearby town and a bunch of us were going down to check it out. I invited Kim to come along. This was not just a concert; the actual concert didn't actually begin until after the performer led worship at this True Love Waits rally. It's funny, looking back on it now, and I'm grateful for the train wreck that occurred, because it changed the way I saw how to present biblical truth to people and how to proclaim holiness in the light of the cross of Jesus. That night, I thought hopefully to myself, "Kim's here, and this guy is going to preach. Maybe this will be how God saves Kim through all this work that we've done in loving her, encouraging her, and walking with her."

The preacher took the stage, and disaster ensued. I don't know how else to describe the sermon. There was very little Bible in it. He gave us a lot of statistics about STDs. There was a lot of, "You don't want syphilis, do you?" and, "It's all fun and games until you've got herpes on your lip." And in the middle of all this moralistic fearmongering, his big illustration was to take out a single red rose. He smelled the rose dramatically on stage, caressed its petals, and talked about how beautiful this rose was and how it had been fresh cut that day. In fact, he said, it was such a beautiful rose that he wanted all of us to see and smell it. So he threw the rose out into the crowd, and he encouraged everyone to pass it around. We were sitting toward the back of the auditorium of a thousand, and it made its way to us, all while he kept preaching. As he neared the end of his message, he asked for the rose back. And, of course, when he got it back in his hands, it was broken and drooping, and the petals were falling off. He held up this now-ugly rose for all to see, and his big finish was this: "Now who in the world would want *this*? Who would want this rose now? Would you be proud of this rose? Is this rose lovely?" His words and his tone were merciless.

I was such an idiot, because, during all that, I'd been praying that Kim was listening. I was praying that Kim would really hear what the preacher was saying about this dirty rose. But there was no real climax to the message. His essential message, which was supposed to represent Jesus's message to a world of sinners, was this: "Hey, don't be a dirty rose."

This approach was dramatically effective in producing shame but not really effective in producing hope. On the way home, Kim was quiet, even though we talked about the concert and what had gone on. I asked her on multiple occasions if everything was okay, if she was all right, and what she thought of the message. Throughout our drive she was quiet, which wasn't like her, but I just thought, naively, that maybe the Holy Spirit was convicting her and that we'd talk about it later when she'd tell me she was a new creation.

Kim continued to act strangely around me for a while. About a week or two later, Kim didn't show up for class. She didn't show up for class for a week. I called and left several messages but couldn't get hold of her. After about three weeks, I began to get nervous. I wondered if she had dropped out of school. She had a dark past, and I wondered if she had fallen back into some of her old habits. Then I got a phone call from a woman who claimed to be Kim's mom. Kim had been in an accident and had been in the hospital right across the street from the university. So I hung up the phone with her mom, and I walked over to her hospital room. She was all bandaged up, and her face was still swollen. She had fallen out of a car that was going 70 miles an hour and had struck her head on the concrete and fractured her skull. The swelling wasn't so extensive as to cause long-term damage, but it did cause enough damage to keep her hospitalized for several weeks.

In the middle of our conversation, seemingly out of nowhere, she asked me, "Do you think I'm a dirty rose?" My heart sank inside of me, and I began to explain to her that the whole weight of the gospel of Jesus Christ is that Jesus wants the rose! It's Jesus's desire to save, redeem, and restore the dirty rose.

Sealed in my heart that day was the truth that unless the gospel is made explicit, unless we clearly articulate that our righteousness is imputed to us by Jesus Christ, that on the cross he absorbed the wrath of God aimed at us and washed us clean—even if we preach biblical words on obeying God—people will believe that Jesus's message is that he has come to condemn the world, not to save it.

But the problem is deeper than that and more pervasive. If we don't make sure the gospel is explicit, if we don't put up the cross and the perfect life of Jesus Christ as our hope, then people can get confused and say, "Yes, I believe in Jesus. I want to be saved. I want to be justified by God," but then begin attempting to earn his salvation. By taking the cross out of the functional equation, moral therapeutic deism promotes the wrong-headed idea that God probably needs our help in the work of justification and most certainly needs us to carry the weight of our sanctification, as well. The result is innumerable Christians suffering under the burden of the law's curse because they have not been led to see that gospel-centered living is the only way to delight in the law.

Grace-Driven Effort

Let's walk through 1 Corinthians 15:1–2. Paul begins, "Now I would remind you, brothers . . ." Who is he talking to? Paul is talking to those who have been justified, those who already believe. "I would remind you, brothers, of the gospel" (v. 1). Paul makes a habit of this. Over and over again he proclaims the gospel to those who *already know that gospel*. He does it in Romans 1:13–15, where he says, "I want you to know, brothers, that I have often intended to come to you (but thus far have been prevented), in order that I may reap some harvest among you. . . . So I am eager to preach the gospel to you also who are in Rome." He does the same thing in Galatians, Ephesians, Philippians, and Colossians. Over and over again he preaches the gospel to people who know the gospel.

Why does he do that? He tells us the answer in 1 Corinthians 15:1–2: "Now I would remind you, brothers, of the gospel I preached to you, which you received [past tense], in which you stand [present tense], and by which you are being saved [future tense]." We see that the gospel had been received, and now it is holding them up. So the gospel not only saves us, but it sustains us.

The remarkable reality reflected here is that the gospel of Jesus Christ—that God saves sinners through the perfect life, substitutionary death, and bodily resurrection of Jesus—justifies us but it also sanctifies us. What do we do, then, with all of the commands of God in Scripture about holiness, purity, and behavioral alignment? D. A. Carson opens this up for us, writing:

> People do not drift toward holiness. Apart from grace-driven effort, people do not gravitate toward godliness, prayer, obedience to Scripture, faith, and delight in the Lord. We drift toward compromise and call it tolerance; we drift toward disobedience and call it freedom; we drift toward superstition and call it faith. We cherish the indiscipline of lost self-control and call it relaxation; we slouch toward prayerlessness and delude ourselves into thinking we have escaped legalism; we slide toward godlessness and convince ourselves we have been liberated.[2]

We are not going to grow in the Christian life through stasis. We must move. It is not an idle life that we live as believers in Christ. But where do we move? And how? What is grace-driven effort, and how is it different from the motivations offered by moralism? What is the difference between moralistic deism and grace-driven effort? There are essentially five components to a right understanding of grace-driven effort, and what they all revolve around is not our religious performance but Christ's saving performance on our behalf. These components revolve around Christ's cross, not our bootstraps.

The Weapons of Grace

First, grace-driven effort uses the weapons of grace. When you're walking in moralistic deism, trying to earn God's favor, and your access to God is built around how well you're behaving, then you are motivated to obey by the hope of acceptance through your behavior. The perverted fruit this produces is something akin to the prosperity gospel. God does not give people cancer because they had only a fifteen-minute quiet time. Nor does God give people health and wealth because they faithfully have that fifteen-minute quiet time. We must abandon the idea that there *is* condemnation for those who are in Christ Jesus! We must abandon the idea that our sins pile up on some scale that will earn God's punishment when tipped, as if Christ didn't take this wrath from us already on the cross. We must also abandon the idea that our good behavior somehow rubs the spiritual lamp that inclines God, like a genie, to emerge and give us the things we wish for.

As a pastor I hear this kind of nonsense all the time. When bad things happen—when a guy loses his job or gets sick—he begins to think of all the ways he has failed God as the reason that the bad things are happening. I also hear the reverse when good things happen: that business deal went through or the girl said yes because I went on a missions trip or I didn't miss a Sunday in church last year. But that's not how grace-driven effort works. A man who understands the gospel and the cross will instead fight sin with the weapons that grace gives us. There are three such weapons.

The first weapon is the blood of Christ. Ephesians 2:13 tells us, "But now in Christ Jesus you who once were far off have been brought near by the blood of Christ." We have been brought near by the blood of Christ. We have not been brought near by our behavior but by the sacrifice of Jesus alone. The marker of those who understand the gospel of Jesus Christ is that, when they stumble and fall, when they screw up, they run *to* God and not *from* him, because they clearly understand that their acceptance before God is not predicated upon their behavior but on the righteous life of Jesus Christ and his sacrificial death.

The second weapon of grace is the Word of God. In 2 Timothy 3:16–17 Paul writes, "All Scripture is breathed out by God and profitable for teaching, for reproof, for correction, and for training in righteousness, that the man of God may be competent, equipped for every good work." When we begin to know the Scriptures well, we can identify what is true and what is a lie. Here is one truth *about truth* to think about: the Holy Spirit and the accusations of the Devil can do the same thing. Both can make us aware of our shortcomings and the impossibility of earning favor with God. The difference between what the Holy Spirit does and what the Devil does is the Spirit's deliverance of the gospel. The Devil brings up gospel truths to accuse and condemn, whereas the Spirit brings up these truths to convict and to comfort. If you are looking at your sins and shortcomings and constantly feeling condemned—not convicted, but condemned—you need to use the Word of God to rebuke the Devil's accusations. You need to use the Word of God to remind yourself over and over again that the gospel is true.

The third weapon of grace is the promise of the new covenant. Hebrews 9:15 says, "He is the mediator of a new covenant, so that those who are called may receive the promised eternal inheritance, since a death has occurred that redeems them from the transgressions committed under the first covenant." To explain the old and new covenants to you in the most simple way I can, let me tell you about an exchange I had when speaking at a church planter's conference held near my hometown. When I was done preaching, I decided to hop in my car, drive twenty minutes to the town in which I grew up, and look at the houses that I remembered from back then. As I drove into town, I passed a field where I once got into a fistfight with a kid named Sean. It was not a fair fight, and I did some shady, dark things in that fight. I completely humiliated him in front of a large crowd of people to the point where, if you were to say my name in front of Sean, wherever he is today, if Christ has not done a work in his life, then I am sure rage would well up in him. Then I drove past my first house, and I thought of all the wicked things I had done in that house. I passed a friend's house where once, at a party, I did some of the most shameful, horrific things that I have ever done.

Afterward, on the drive back up to the conference, I was overwhelmed with the guilt and shame of the wickedness that I had done in that city prior to knowing Jesus Christ (and some *after* I came to know him). I could hear the whispers in my heart: "You call yourself a man of God? Are you going to stand in front of these guys and tell them to be men of God? After all you've done?"

Now, watch the three weapons of grace collide. In the middle of all that guilt and shame, I began to be reminded by the Scriptures that the old Matt Chandler is dead. The Matt Chandler who did those things, the Matt Chandler who sinned in those ways, was nailed to that cross with Jesus Christ, and all of his sins—past, present, and future—were paid for in full on the cross of Jesus Christ. I have been sanctified "once for all" (Heb. 10:10). He remembers my sins no more (Heb. 8:12). And I no longer need to feel shame for those things, because those things have been completely atoned for.

When we fight sin, we don't do so with our own unction. We fight sin with the weapons that grace gives us: the blood of Jesus Christ, the Word of God, and the promise of the new covenant, that Christ has paid for our shortcomings in obedience to the law by his perfect life imputed to us. That fight is the first component of grace-driven effort.

The Roots, Not the Branches

Second, a grace-driven effort attacks the roots of our sin, not just the branches. Grace is a heart changer, because the heart is where behavior comes from. Wherever our heart is, that is where our actions will follow. We can manage our behavior until the cows come home and never have a God-loving heart, which is how the Pharisees lived.

Let me get specific. There is a reason you have a pornography issue. Someone may return to pornography again and again, and this is likely not because he just really likes sex. We're wired by God to really like sex. That's just barely scratching the surface of the problem with pornography. Right underneath the desire for pleasure is lust, but the reality is that, nine times out of ten, pornography problems are not just about lust. It runs deeper than that too. Lust is a symptom of a more central perversion of the heart.

Men, there is a heart-based reason that you're a miserable husband and father. Ladies, there is a heart-based reason that you constantly have to tear down other women and feel led to point out their flaws and failures. There is a reason this stuff is happening. The roots are bad; they are producing bad fruit.

Grace-driven effort wants to get to the bottom of behavior, not just manage behavior. If you're simply managing behavior but not removing the roots of that behavior, then the weeds simply sprout up in another place. You may mow it down for a season of time only to see it sprout up again. Pink (the theologian, not the singer) is instructive:

> True mortification consists, first, in weakening sin's root and principle. It is of little avail to chop off the heads of weeds while their roots remain in the ground; nor is much accomplished by seeking to correct outward habits while the heart be left neglected. One in a high fever cannot expect to lower his temperature while he continues to eat heartily, nor can the lusts of the flesh be weakened so long as we feed or "make provision for" (Rom. 13:14) them.[3]

Grace-driven effort not only uses the weapons of grace, but it also attacks the roots, not just the branches, whereas moralism tries just to subdue behavior. Moralism says, "I've got a pornography issue. Here's what I need to do to stop looking at pornography: install filters, tell a friend who will punch me when I mess up, and maybe even throw away my computer if none of that works." Now, obviously, there's nothing wrong with safeguards. You won't solve an alcoholic's problems by taking the booze out of his kitchen, but you should still take the booze out of his kitchen. But when all is said and done, if we don't kill the root of sin, we will keep seeing the branches of sin. So grace-driven effort wants to answer the desire, the affections at the heart of what results in use of pornography or alcoholism. What exactly are we medicating with those sins? What are we trying to escape or avoid? And how does the gospel fill those needs?

The use of pornography, for instance, may result from root

feelings of shame. As we meditate on the gospel truth that Jesus covers our shame, that he himself is not ashamed to call us his brothers and sisters, we cultivate new affections for him rather than for the deadening substitute of pornography. The abuse of alcohol can result from all kinds of pain: brokenness traced to childhood trauma, patterns developed in early seasons of rebellion, or a deep-seated need to escape from all kinds of personal problems. Even as we seek practical help to prevent physically drinking, we ought also to shine the light of the gospel over and over again into these dark recesses of our soul. The gospel declares that we are reconciled to a perfect Father whose love for us is unwavering and eternal. The gospel wins us to allegiance to Christ, forgiving us for all rebellion and making us prisoners of hope and slaves to righteousness. The gospel brings hope for healing from all manner of hurts. Knowing this, and more, we are better equipped to combat idolatry with the real cure, not just superficial behavior modification.

We're after heart change, not just a conformity to a pattern of religion. We're looking for a transformation by the Holy Spirit's power.

Fear of God

Grace-driven effort fights for a reason that goes beyond a clear conscience and an emotional peace. One of the things I run into over and over again in my counseling role is people who are broken over sin in their life, but as I begin to dig around in there, most of the time, they're not broken up because they have sinned against a holy God. They are broken up because their sin is costing them something. They've been busted. In his great mercy, God has outed their secrets. A spouse has left them. Or in some way, they are just hurting from the painful consequences of sin. But when it gets down to it, they are really just sorry they got caught. They are really just sorry something bad is happening. They are what 2 Corinthians 7:10 would call "in a state of worldly sorrow." They are sorrowful that their rebellion against God has led to these consequences in their life, but they have no real understanding that they have defamed and dishonored God himself.

They have slandered his name and sinned against him. But that's not their chief concern. They see their sin as making life difficult for themselves, but they are not appalled at all at how they have slandered the God of the universe. These people somehow don't understand that when we sin, we sin against God.

David clearly saw this in his sin against God after arranging the murder of Uriah, with whose wife, Bathsheba, he had committed adultery. Despite defiling those two people, he confessed out loud to the Lord, "Against you, you only, have I sinned" (Ps. 51:4). Surely he sinned against Uriah. Surely there was collateral damage around that sin, but David's understanding was first and foremost, "I have sinned against you, God"; his heart was grieved about his rebellion against God, not just about the consequences of his actions. Grace-driven effort has in view not just peace of mind but a restoration to the holiness of God and the cause of God's glory.

Dead to Sin

Fourth, grace-driven effort doesn't just forsake sin but is absolutely *dead* to it. The believer pursuing holiness by grace-driven effort is not going to serve sin, because he is alive to God. This is the difference between what the Puritans would call "vivification" and "mortification." What ends up happening to so many of us is that we spend so much time trying to put sin to death that we don't spend enough time striving to know God deeply, trying to gaze upon the wonder of Jesus Christ and have that transform our affections to the point where our love and hope are steadfastly on Christ. The goal is this: that Christ would become more beautiful and desirable than the allure of sin.

In the church I grew up in, we would sing:

Turn your eyes upon Jesus.
Look full in his wonderful face.

And the things of this earth will grow strangely dim
In the light of his glory and grace.[4]

Those are great words. Do you hear what's happening there? As we turn our eyes toward Jesus Christ and gaze upon him, as we really *see* Jesus and behold him, as we become enraptured in his infinite beauties and perfections, then the things of the world grow dim and begin by contrast to lose their power over our heart and life. Christ becomes what we really desire, and earthly things become dead to us and unworthy of our affections. John Owen writes:

> Herein would I live; herein would I die; hereon would I dwell in my thoughts and affections, to the withering and consumption of all the painted beauties of this world, unto the crucifying all things here below, until they become unto me a dead and deformed thing, no way meet for affectionate embraces. For these and the like reasons, I shall first inquire into our beholding of the glory of Christ in this world by faith.[5]

Owen knows that to crucify himself to the things of the world, he must "first inquire" into the beauty of Jesus.

Moralism doesn't do that. The moralist tends to forsake sin so that God might love him, so that he might earn the favor of God. All of his effort and striving become his foundation of hope and comfort. And it simply doesn't work. If anything, it's shame upon shame upon shame as we continue to fail.

Gospel Violence

Here's the fifth and last component of grace-driven effort, distinguishing the gospel from moralism. Grace-driven effort is violent. It is aggressive. The person who understands the gospel understands that, as a new creation, his spiritual nature is in opposition to sin now, and he seeks not just to weaken sin in his life but to outright destroy it. Out of love for Jesus, he wants sin starved to death, and he will hunt and pursue the death of every sin in his heart until he has achieved success. This is a very different pursuit than simply wanting to be good. It is the result of having transferred one's affections to Jesus. When God's love takes hold of us, it powerfully pushes out our own love for other gods and frees our love to flow back to him in true worship. And when we love God, we obey him.

The moralist doesn't operate that way. While true obedience is a result of love, moralistic legalism assumes it works the other way around, that love results from obedience. From the standpoint of moralistic legalism, root issues aren't of utmost importance; appearing obedient is. The moralist is far more interested in external actions, which still gives sin quarters in his heart. Moralistic, therapeutic deism is fine with sin hiding in a foxhole. The gospel wants to nuke the hole. As long as bad behavior is not visible or tangible, the moralist will tolerate some of what Jerry Bridges calls "respectable sins."[6] A moralist is not on the hunt; he's not aggressively seeking to destroy that which is evil in him but is content to simply wash his hands.

We host a family camp every year at our church. It's up in the Ozarks, and they have a petting zoo there. I'll be honest: this is a ghetto petting zoo. There is a sad-looking llama there and some of those fainting goats—if you make a loud sound, their defense mechanism is just to fall over like they're dead. When we get to that part of the petting zoo, we're told, "Please don't jack with the goats. Please leave them alone. Please don't freak them out." What do you think happens? Every year, even though we can all see posted on a sign that we are not to jack with the goats, and even though some person giving us the orientation tour is telling us not to jack with the goats, you can see the thought form in the minds of countless men filing in. They're thinking to themselves, "I really want to jack with these goats." So of course by the end of the orientation, the men of our church—wicked men—have usually constructed a bracket of some kind and devised a scoring system to rank who's best at knocking these goats out. They clap their hands and scream, smacking the goats on the bottom and trying to do whatever they can to get these goats to black out. I've thought to myself every year, "Man, it would be interesting if these were fainting lions, not goats." Do you think guys are going to slap a lion in its backside, scream in front of its face, or chase it around? No, because a lion is an apex predator. It was created by God to eat whatever it wants to eat. These dudes wouldn't jack with a lion like they would with a goat.

When we think we are dealing only with a so-called respectable sin, we think we're just handling a fainting goat when we're actually jacking with a lion. Think of TV shows such as *When Animals Attack*. I find myself at times rooting for the animals simply because the people are so dumb. The witnesses in the videos are always saying things like, "I can't believe it happened." But I think, "I can believe it happened. It's a *lion*. That's what it does. That's what it was created to do."

People who understand the gospel of Jesus Christ seek to put sin to death because they understand that sin is a lion and will eventually destroy and devour them. By grace and in grace we scour every corner of our hearts, every square inch of our lives, and probe our minds to find anything that is not in submission to Jesus Christ, and we eradicate it altogether for the glory of God, for the safety of our soul, and for the love of those around us.

The True Heart of the Father

There is a magical thing that happens in homes all over the world. When you have a child, you want your child to crawl, and then you want your kid to walk. My first child, Audrey, pulled herself to the coffee table. When she got to the coffee table, she began to bounce on her knees, and then she began to coast along. From there she started letting go and just being wobbly. At that point we began to get excited about the fact that Audrey was about to walk. Eventually she took her hands off of the coffee table, and we watched physics in motion.

God has created children, specifically young children, with

gargantuan heads and tiny little bodies. So when Audrey let go of the coffee table, her gigantic head fell forward, and suddenly she had a decision to make. She could stick that foot out to catch herself or she could die. So she stuck her foot out, and then she had momentum. It was step, step, step, fall. Do you know what we did? We exploded in celebration. We picked her up, spun her around, and kissed her face. Then we sat her down and pleaded with her to walk toward us again. After that we began e-mailing, Facebooking, taking pictures, tweeting, and all sorts of other things to get the word out that Audrey was walking. We did that with our son, Reid, and we've done that with our daughter Norah.

What I have learned as I watched all of our friends have children is that there is always an epic celebration around the kid walking. This is news to be declared. "This kid is walking!"

For all the people I have watched go through that process, I've never seen anybody watch their kid go step, step, step, fall and then say out loud, "Man, this kid is an idiot. Are you serious? Just three steps? Man, I can get the dog to walk two or three steps. Honey, this must be from your side of the family, because my side of the family is full of walkers. This must be some sort of genetic, shallow gene pool on your side of things."

No father does that. Every father rejoices in the steps of his child. The father celebrates the steps of his child. I think what we have here is a picture of God celebrating us walking. So we step, step, step, and fall, and heaven applauds. At what? At the obedience of taking those three steps. The Father in heaven is crying, "He's walking!" "She's doing it!" And maybe the Accuser's saying, "No, he only took a couple of steps. That's nothing."

But the celebration is in the steps, even if there are still falls. Here's what I know about all of my children: they start to walk farther and farther and farther, and they begin to skip, they begin to run, they begin to jump, they begin to climb, and they begin to tear the house *up*. It's beautiful. I knew even when they were step, step, step, falling that that process was the beginning of what would result in climbing trees, dancing, and sprinting. Knowing in my mind what's to come, the three steps and the stumble were a celebration.

Moralists see the fall and believe that the Father is ashamed and thinks they're foolish. So, more often than not, they stop trying to walk because they can't see the Father rejoicing in and celebrating his child.

Church of Jesus, let us please be men and women who understand the difference between moralism and the gospel of Jesus Christ. Let's be careful to preach the dos and don'ts of Scripture in the shadow of the cross's "Done!" Resolve to know nothing but Jesus Christ crucified. We are not looking to conform people to a pattern of religion but pleading with the Holy Spirit to transform people's lives. Let us move forward according to that upward call, holding firmly to the explicit gospel.

What we see in the Father's heart in the Bible is its immensity, its bottomless depths. God's heart is as complex and unfathomable as he is. Shouldn't we stand firm in the gospel we believe and proclaim so that we reflect the bigness of God's heart for a fallen world? The cross of Christ and his resurrection are cataclysms of the unsearchable judgments and affections of God. It is this immense gospel that spurs Paul to pray:

> For this reason I bow my knees before the Father, from whom every family in heaven and on earth is named, that according to the riches of his glory he may grant you to be strengthened with power through his Spirit in your inner being, so that Christ may dwell in your hearts through faith—that you, being rooted and grounded in love, may have strength to comprehend with all the saints what is the breadth and length and height and depth, and to know the love of Christ that surpasses knowledge, that you may be filled with all the fullness of God. (Eph. 3:14–19)

The Scripture's complementary perspectives of the gospel on the ground and the gospel in the air help us comprehend the breadth, length, height, and depth of God's love. Neither perspective dilutes the other but rather shapes our vision of God's saving purposes to the epic scope of biblical revelation. We are after a gospel that is resolutely centered on the atoning work of Christ and scaled to the glory of God. Let the explicit gospel drive us to worship with all "the fullness of God" (Eph. 3:19) and in awe of both God's immense, universe-subsuming glory and his deep, personal love for sinners. May we never *assume* that people understand this gospel but, instead, let's faithfully live out and faithfully proclaim the explicit gospel with all the energy and compassion our great God and King has graciously given.

Appendix:
The Gospel Assumed
or Explicit?

Is the gospel assumed in your relationships? Or is the gospel explicit? I have been thinking about this distinction for a few days now. Those who live life under the banner of an assumed gospel simply navigate the waters of life with an underlying foundation that is personal and meaningful. An assumed gospel often means that a person deeply values the gospel and tries to live life according to the gospel.

The issue with an assumed gospel is that it is often too personal and, therefore, becomes private. People who live under the assumption of the gospel often know how it relates to their life, but nobody else does. Their kids never see how the gospel affects decisions, arguments, finances, etc. Their neighbors never hear of the hope within. Their coworkers are left to wonder about what makes them different. Those who live under the assumed gospel often find it awkward to bring it up and talk about the work of Christ. Why? Because they never bring it up and learn to articulate the implications of Christ's atoning work and their life.

On the contrary, those who are explicit about the gospel in their relationships have a different effect. By living out the gospel and speaking about the gospel and working through the gospel (verbally), they are helping to connect the dots for those around them. Their kids hear how the gospel relates to the family finances or time or relationships or arguments. Their neighbors hear about the hope within. Coworkers are privy to the reality that this person is not simply a moral guy or girl, but one who is forgiven and transformed by the death and resurrection of Christ.

I want to encourage you to begin and, with some of you, continue to make the gospel explicit in your relationships. Don't waste life by living an assumed gospel; rather, flesh it out and connect the dots for yourself and those around you. Talk with your spouse about how Christ's person and work relates to everything. Pass this on to your kids. Mention Christ. Talk about Christ. Point to Christ. Relate to Christ. Oftentimes where the gospel is assumed, it is quickly lost.

Josh Patterson[1]

Notes

Introduction

1. Dave Harvey, *When Sinners Say "I Do"* (Wapwallopen, PA: Shepherd's Press, 2007), 24.

2. Not her real name.

3. Christian Smith with Melinda Lundquist Denton, *Soul Searching: The Religious and Spiritual Lives of American Teenagers* (Oxford: Oxford University Press, 2009), 118.

4. I have taken the title "The Explicit Gospel" from Josh Patterson, who is one of the lead pastors at The Village. He wrote a short blog by the same title a couple of years ago. You can view that blog in the appendix.

Chapter 1: God

1. James S. Stewart, *A Faith to Proclaim* (Vancouver, BC: Regent College Press, 2002), 102.

2. In Texas, keeping livestock on your land results in an agricultural exemption from some taxes.

3. Abraham Kuyper, "Sphere Sovereignty," in *Abraham Kuyper: A Centennial Reader*, ed. James D. Bratt (Grand Rapids, MI: Eerdmans, 1998), 488.

4. "Thus, while all the Bible is not about us, it is all for us." Herbert Lockyer, *The Holy Spirit of God* (Nashville, TN: Abingdon, 1983), 59.

5. The easy charge of "prooftexting" often comes from those who don't like another's conclusion.

6. John Piper, *God's Passion for His Glory: Living the Vision of Jonathan Edwards* (Wheaton, IL: Crossway, 1998), 32.

7. Ibid.

Chapter 2: Man

1. And here we see an instance where God's kindness and severity are not mutually exclusive.

2. In this survey of what it means to view the gospel from the ground, we can notice clearly the falling short of God's glory that each person is culpable of. In chapter 6, when we view the gospel from the air, we will be able to survey the cosmic and historical origins of this culpability.

3. John Piper, "The Echo and the Insufficiency of Hell, Part 2," sermon preached at Bethlehem Baptist Church, Minneapolis (June 21, 1992), http://www.desiringgod.org/ResourceLibrary/Sermons/BySeries/20/801_The_Echo_and_Insufficiency_of_Hell_Part_2/.

4. Thomas Watson, *The Doctrine of Repentance* (Carlisle, PA: Banner of Truth, 1988), 63.

Chapter 3: Christ

1. The word *gospel* comes from the Koine Greek word *evangelion*, which means "good news" or "glad tidings."

2. See especially Martin Hengel, *Crucifixion in the Ancient World and the Folly of the Cross* (Philadelphia: Fortress, 1977).

3. Cathy Lynn Grossman, "Has the 'Notion of Sin' Been Lost?," *USA Today Online* (April 16, 2008), http://www.usatoday.com/news/religion/2008-03-19-sin_N.htm.

Chapter 4: Response

1. Chan Kilgore, "Mission," sermon, Resurgence Conference, Orlando, Florida (February 2, 2011), http://theresurgence.com/2011/03/31/chan-kilgore-mission.

2. Michael Spencer, *Mere Churchianity: Finding Your Way Back to Jesus-Shaped Spirituality* (Colorado Springs, CO: Waterbrook, 2010), 51.

3. We will discuss this danger more fully in chapter 9, "Dangers in a Gospel on the Ground Too Long."

4. Charles Spurgeon, "The Necessity of the Spirit's Work," in *Sermons Preached and Revised by the Rev. C. H. Spurgeon*, 6th Series (New York: Sheldon, 1860), 188.

5. Just one example is Lydia's response to the gospel: "The Lord opened her heart to pay attention to what was said by Paul" (Acts 16:14).

6. This is a danger we will explore more fully in chapter 10, "Dangers in a Gospel in the Air Too Long."

7. D. A. Carson, *Scandalous: The Cross and Resurrection of Jesus* (Wheaton, IL: Crossway, 2010), 105–6.

Chapter 5: Creation

1. D. Martyn Lloyd-Jones, *Preaching and Preachers* (Grand Rapids, MI: Zondervan, 1972), 68–69.

2. Joe Schwarcz, *That's the Way the Cookie Crumbles: 62 All-New Commentaries on the Fascinating Chemistry of Everyday Life* (Toronto: ECW Press, 2002), 21–22.

3. Jonah Lehrer, "Accept Defeat: The Neuroscience of Screwing Up," *Wired* (December 21, 2009), http://www.wired.com/magazine/2009/12/fail_accept_defeat/all/1.

4. Jonah Lehrer, "The Truth Wears Off: Is There Something Wrong with the Scientific Method?," *The New Yorker* (December 13, 2010), http://www.newyorker.com/reporting/2010/12/13/101213fa_fact_lehrer?currentPage=all.

5. Quoted in Carl F. H. Henry, "Theology and Science," in *God Who Speaks and Shows: Preliminary Considerations,* vol. 1, God, Revelation and Authority (Wheaton, IL: Crossway, 1999), 170.

6. Ibid., 175.

7. Douglas F. Kelly, *Creation and Change: Genesis 1:1–2:4 in the Light of Changing Scientific Paradigms* (Ross-shire, UK: Christian Focus, 1997), 63.

8. See the valuable survey of Robert Letham, "'In the Space of Six Days': The Days of Creation from Origen to the Westminster Assembly," *Westminster Theological Journal* 61 (1999): 147–74, which is helpfully summarized by Justin Taylor, "How Did the Church Interpret the Days of Creation before Darwin?," Between Two Worlds weblog (February 14, 2011), http://thegospelcoalition.org/blogs/justintaylor/2011/02/14/how-did-the-church-interpret-the-days-of-creation-before-darwin/.

9. But you could check out, for instance, Michael Behe, *Darwin's Black Box: The Biochemical Challenge to Evolution* (New York: Simon & Schuster, 1996), or Stephen Meyer, *Signature in the Cell: DNA and the Evidence for Intelligent Design* (New York: HarperCollins, 2009).

10. Phillip E. Johnson, *The Wedge of Truth: Splitting the Foundations of Naturalism* (Downers Grove, IL: InterVarsity, 2000), 151–52.

11. Ibid., 152.

12. Mark Driscoll, "Answers to Common Questions about Creation," The Resurgence Online (July 3, 2006), http://theresurgence.com/2006/07/03/answers-to-common-questions-about-creation.

13. Timothy Keller, *Counterfeit Gods: The Empty Promises of Money, Sex, and Power, and the Only Hope That Matters* (New York: Dutton, 2009), *xviii*; emphasis original.

14. John Calvin, *Institutes of the Christian Religion,* 1.5.1, trans. Ford Lewis Battles, ed. John T. McNeill (Philadelphia: Westminster, 1960), 52.

15. Rick Warren, *The Purpose-Driven Life* (Grand Rapids, MI: Zondervan, 2002), 17.

Chapter 6: Fall

1. R. C. Sproul, *The Holiness of God* (Carol Stream, IL: Tyndale, 1998), 116.

2. Cornelius Plantinga Jr., *Not the Way It's Supposed to Be: A Breviary of Sin* (Grand Rapids, MI: Eerdmans, 1995), 10; emphasis original.

3. Timothy Keller, *The Reason for God: Belief in an Age of Skepticism* (New York: Dutton, 2008), 170.

4. Herman Melville, *Moby Dick* (Boston: Simonds, 1922), 400.

5. You can view the gallery of Demotivators at http://www.despair.com/viewall.html.

6. Quoted in Keller, *The Reason for God,* 162.

7. Quoted in Miranda Wilcox, "Exilic Imagining in *The Seafarer* and *The Lord of the Rings*," in *Tolkien the Medievalist*, ed. Jane Chance (New York: Routledge, 2003), 138.

8. Blaise Pascal, *Thoughts*, trans. W. F. Trotter (New York: Collier, 1910), 138.

9. C. S. Lewis, "Answers to Questions on Christianity," in *"God in the Dock": Essays on Theology and Ethics* (Grand Rapids, MI: Eerdmans, 1993), 58.

10. C. S. Lewis, "The Weight of Glory," in *"The Weight of Glory": And Other Addresses* (New York: HarperCollins, 2001), 26.

11. Ibid.

12. Ibid.

13. Pascal, *Thoughts*, 138–39.

Chapter 7: Reconciliation

1. It is for this reason that I have labeled this plot point in the "In the Air" narrative *reconciliation* rather than the more common *redemption*.

2. I first heard this "concentric circle" idea in a sermon Mark Dever preached at a 9Marks conference at SEBTS in 2010, http://www.9marks.org/audio/9marks-southeastern-2010-mark-dever.

3. The precise origin of the terms *attractional* and *missional* is uncertain, but certainly two of the first popularizers—if not *the* first popularizers—of the way the terms are used today are Michael Frost and Alan Hirsch, beginning with their book *The Shaping of Things to Come: Innovation and Mission for the 21st-Century Church* (Grand Rapids, MI: Baker, 2004).

4. Abraham Kuyper, "Sphere Sovereignty," in *Abraham Kuyper: A Centennial Reader*, ed. James D. Bratt (Grand Rapids, MI: Eerdmans, 1998), 461; emphasis added.

Chapter 8: Consummation

1. John Newton, "Amazing Grace" (1760–1770). The lyrics quoted, however, comprise the hymn's last stanza, which many attribute to an unknown author.

2. William Featherston, "My Jesus, I Love Thee" (1864).

3. Anthony A. Hoekema, *The Bible and the Future* (Grand Rapids, MI: Eerdmans, 1994), 275.

4. Augustine, *The City of God*, XXII.30, trans. Marcus Dods (New York: Random House, 1950), 864–65.

5. N. T. Wright, *Surprised by Hope: Rethinking Heaven, the Resurrection, and the Mission of the Church* (New York: HarperCollins, 2008), 104–5.

6. Ibid., 105–6.

Chapter 10: Dangers in a Gospel in the Air Too Long

1. This lamentable cliché is usually attributed to St. Francis of Assissi, and apart from the theological bankruptcy of the idea, another problem is

that St. Francis never said it. See Mark Galli, "*Speak* the Gospel," *Christianity Today* Online (May 21, 2009), http://www.christianitytoday.com/ct/2009/mayweb-only/120-42.0.html.

2. Rob Bell, *Love Wins: A Book about Heaven, Hell, and the Fate of Every Person Who Ever Lived* (New York: HarperOne, 2011).

Chapter 11: Moralism and the Cross

1. Ned Flanders is the goody-two-shoes Christian neighbor on the TV program *The Simpsons*.

2. D. A. Carson, *For the Love of God: A Daily Companion for Discovering the Riches of God's Word*, vol. 2 (Wheaton, IL: Crossway, 1999), 23.

3. Arthur W. Pink, *The Holy Spirit* (Mulberry, IN: Sovereign Grace, 2002), 106.

4. Helen Lemmel, "Turn Your Eyes upon Jesus" (1922).

5. John Owen, *The Glorious Mystery of the Person of Christ, God and Man* (New York: Robert Carter, 1839), 381.

6. Jerry Bridges, *Respectable Sins: Confronting the Sins We Tolerate* (Colorado Springs, CO: NavPress, 2007).

Appendix

1. Josh Patterson, "The Gospel Assumed, or Explicit?," August 4, 2009, http://fm.thevillagechurch.net/blog/pastors/?p=308.

General Index

sin, 43, 50, 59–60, 109–13, 120–21, 135, 205, 215–19
Smith, Christian, 13
social gospel, 189, 193
Social Gospel Movement, 192–93
social justice, 149–52, 191
sorrow, 215–16
Spencer, Michael, 72
Spurgeon, Charles, 77–78
success, 114–15
suffering, 46
syncretism, 189–91

Tolkien, J. R. R., 121
total depravity, 107–9, 131

Warren, Rick, 105
Watson, Thomas, 50
wealth, 120
Westminster Confession of Faith, 34–36

wisdom, 33, 114–15, 119–20, 124–25
Word of God, 70–71, 194–95, 211–12
work, 117–18
works, 64–68, 176, 190
world, 189–91
worship, 35–37, 39–40, 49, 51, 103–5
Wright, N. T., 170–71

Scripture Index

 # RE:LIT

Resurgence Literature (Re:Lit) is a ministry of the Resurgence. At theResurgence.com you will find free theological resources in blog, audio, video, and print forms, along with information on forthcoming conferences, to help Christians contend for and contextualize Jesus's gospel. At ReLit.org you will also find the full lineup of Resurgence books for sale. The elders of Mars Hill Church have generously agreed to support Resurgence and the Acts 29 Church Planting Network in an effort to serve the entire church.

FOR MORE RESOURCES

Re:Lit – relit.org
Resurgence – theResurgence.com
Re:Train – retrain.org
Mars Hill Church – marshill.com
Acts 29 – acts29network.org

RE:LIT

CHECK OUT SOME OTHER GREAT RE:LIT TITLES

These resources communicate the essential truths about God and life, equipping you to put knowledge and passion into action.

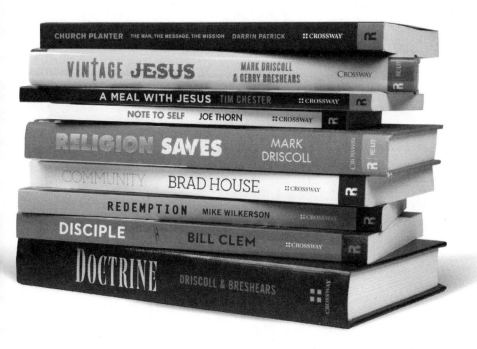

crossway.org/relit

R RESURGENCE

Resurgence Publishing is a ministry of Mars Hill Church. The mission of Resurgence is growing leaders to grow churches. Visit theresurgence.com for more gospel-centered resources.